D0946630

The Earl of Baltimore

Books by

Terry Pluto

THE GREATEST SUMMER

SUPER JOE (with Joe Charboneau and Burt Graeff)

The Story of Earl Weaver, Baltimore Orioles Manager

By Terry Pluto

NEW CENTURY PUBLISHERS, INC.

Copyright © 1982 by Terry Pluto

Cover design copyright © 1982 by New Century Publishers, Inc.

All rights reserved. No part of this book may be used or re-
produced in any manner whatsoever without prior written permission from the publisher except in the case of brief quotations
embodied in critical reviews and articles. All inquiries should
be addressed to New Century Publishers, Inc., 275 Old New Brunswick
Road, Piscataway, New Jersey 08854.
Printing Code
11   12   13   14   15   16

Library of Congress Cataloging in Publication Data

Pluto, Terry, 1955–
  The Earl of Baltimore.

  Includes index.
  1. Weaver, Earl, 1930–   2. Baseball—
United States—Managers—Biography. 3. Baltimore
Orioles (Baseball team) I. Title.
GV865.W38P59   796.357′092′4 [B]   82-2200
ISBN 0-8329-0125-3

To Bert

Contents

Preface

I first met Earl Weaver in February of 1979. I left the *Savannah* (Ga.) *Morning News* where I had spent the summer of 1978 covering the Class AA Savannah Braves. *Baltimore Evening Sun* sports editor Bill Tanton, a man who loves to nurture young writers, found me deep in the Southern League and asked me if I would like to cover the Baltimore Orioles for his paper. I was honored, stunned and scared all at once. That did not stop me from quickly saying "Yes."

"Okay, you report to Miami in two weeks and pick up the Orioles," Tanton told me.

"I want to know one thing," I said to Tanton, "What about Earl Weaver? I mean, he always looks so angry."

Don't worry," said Tanton. "Earl is the greatest. Covering him will be an experience you'll never forget."

Tanton was right. I was in for something special and I could tell it from the start. On the first day of training camp, I asked Weaver a question about building confidence in players.

"I can see right now you need some help," Earl said to me. "You are one of those psychology guys. Well, lesson No. 1 is psychology don't mean anything in baseball and I don't ever want to hear you ask me about momentum. Ain't no such thing. Write that down and remember it. Right now, you don't know what you're doing. If you listen, I'll make a baseball writer out of you after a year. But looking at you, Pluto, I can see it ain't gonna be easy."

If anyone made a baseball writer out of me, it was Weaver. He was patient with my absurd questions and always willing to give advice. As Tanton had said, Earl is the greatest.

Even though Weaver had absolutely nothing to do with this book, I owe him a lot. A rookie writer could not ask for a better manager to cover than Earl Weaver. For that, I am forever grateful.

I would also like to thank Bill Tanton, Ken Nigro, Bob Brown, Harding Christ, and my parents for their support. A special tip of the hat goes to Roberta Pluto for typing the manuscript, Sheldon Ocker for his helpful suggestions, and to George Wieser, my agent, whose relentless efforts made this book possible.

Terry Pluto

1

Earl and Reggie

It was all because of a lousy necktie. Some made it out to be World War III. Others said it was just Earl being Earl and Reggie being Reggie and they both were being a bit pigheaded.

The scene in 1976 was this:

Baltimore Orioles Manager Earl Weaver was playing cards with his coaches. Weaver was in a plane sitting on the runway at Milwaukee Airport. It was a charter flight preparing to wing the Birds to the next stop on their trek across the American League. There was nothing special about this night.

Most of the players were already on the plane when Reggie Jackson came aboard. Weaver glanced up from his cards. He put them down and sprinted to Jackson at the front of the plane.

"Reggie, you ain't getting on the plane," said Weaver.

"Why not?" asked Jackson.

"No tie."

"I don't have a tie with me," said Jackson.

"If you don't have a tie, you don't fly with us," said Weaver.

At this point, most of the Orioles' eyes were riveted on the confrontation between Earl and Reggie. Jackson had just joined the Orioles and this was his first trip with the team. He had the reputation of a guy who was big, bigger than his teammates and bigger than his manager. He didn't want only to star, he demanded to be The Star. The Orioles are a team of restrained egos. They are good and they know it, but they also realize that they need each other to succeed. They are a club of which the whole is greater than the parts, and they wondered what Jackson would do to their chemistry.

As they watched Earl and Reggie argue the merits of wearing a tie, they could hardly wait to see who would win this battle of wills. Reggie stood with hands on hips, glaring at Earl. Catcher Dave Duncan was next to him.

"The deal is this," Weaver explained slowly. "Unless you got a tie, you don't fly."

Jackson and Duncan walked off the airplane into the terminal. About ten minutes later, Reggie returned. He had purchased a tie at one of the airport shops and put it on for Weaver. He then sat down in the aircraft and prepared to leave with the team.

"A lot of managers would have been afraid to challenge Reggie in that situation," said Orioles Scout Jim Russo. "I was on that flight. Reggie had come to us after a long holdout. He was a superstar and this was his new team. You know, I never saw Earl move any faster than he did from that card game to Reggie."

Russo spoke with Jackson the next day.

"I saw Reggie in the hotel lobby," recalled Russo. "He was wearing a tie. We had a rule back then that all players had to wear a coat and tie in the hotel and on flights. Reggie asked me why Earl was so hard on him. I told him it was nothing personal. Rules are rules. Besides, it was club policy, not Earl's rule."

"But Jim, what do I do if it is 95 degrees?" Jackson asked.

"You do the same thing Brooks and Frank Robinson did, you wear a coat and a tie," said Russo.

The scout then grabbed Reggie's tie and turned it over.

"I saw from the label that it was one of those $35 jobs," said Russo. "I told Reggie that he probably had 25 of those. I said, 'Reggie, you were just doing that to test Earl.' Reggie just grinned. Then I told him that it wouldn't do any good. I think Reggie knew it, too."

No matter if it is telling Reggie Jackson to put on a tie, or Jim Palmer to grow up or Ron Luciano to read the rulebook, Earl Weaver comes on like he knows he is the best damn manager in baseball. If you don't believe it, look it up. No active manager has a better winning percentage than Earl Weaver. He has won 60% of his games since taking over the Orioles midway through the 1968 season. Detroit's Sparky Anderson is second in the won–lost race followed by Tom Lasorda, Billy Martin, and Bill Virdon, in that order. In baseball history, only Joe McCarthy has won games at a faster rate than Weaver.

In 13 full years of managing, he has won six division titles.

"For a while there, I thought I was going to slip under .500," Weaver said after his club clinched the 1979 Eastern Division pennant.

Some managers worry about winning half of their games, Weaver is concerned about taking a title every two years.

After the strike-marred 1981 season, Weaver's Orioles have finished first or second in 12 of the 14 years he has been in charge. He has won 100 games a season five times and has run the same team for a longer period than any other active manager. The beat goes on.

Clearly, his record makes Earl a hot commodity, but it is his temper, his inner constitution, and his wit which have made him a star and the game's resident genius. Winning is fine, but it can be boring unless it is done with flair. Houston manager Bill Virdon is among the game's top skippers, yet he is virtually unheralded. Why? He has a personality best colored off-white.

Earl is another story. Often his face is red with anger. Occasionally, his language is blue, and he has been known to turn white when one of his players does something unthinkable on the field. You can color Weaver red, white, and blue, as American as baseball. *Sports Illustrated* writer Frank Deford once suggested that, "Earl Weaver is baseball."

Perhaps. At least, he is baseball at its best and most fun. He is a brilliant strategist and a winner. A legend. He is also, "baseball's Son of Sam," according to umpire Jim Evans. Including 1981, Weaver has been ejected from 81 major league games—an average of seven per season. Three times his conduct with umpires has led to suspensions. But none of this includes Earl's minor league escapades.

"I remember one game where Earl was really mad at the umps," said veteran Minor League Manager Frank Lucchesi. "He is out there stomping and yelling. Suddenly, he grabs his heart and hits the ground like he had an attack or passed out. One of his players starts fanning him with a cap. There was a photographer next to my dugout. I grabbed his camera and ran out on the field to take some pictures. It was a great scene."

Does that make him Son of Sam? Hardly. More like Mickey Rooney.

Then there is Jim Palmer, who often sees nothing humorous about Weaver. In fact, Palmer has said, "Earl doesn't know the difference between a slider and a curve." Dave McNally once said, "The only thing Earl knows about pitching is that he can't hit it." These two pitchers have accounted for more than 30% of Earl's wins in Baltimore.

"Earl Weaver is so good," says Yankee owner George Steinbrenner. "He is ahead of everyone on the field. He is a great manager and a master intimidator of umpires. The last thing they want to see coming from the dugout in front of a home crowd is Weaver. He just plain scares them. In 1980, Reggie [Jackson] batted just .120 in a big series in Baltimore because Earl neutralized him. If that isn't taking the tank, I don't know what is. But part of it was Weaver."

"I don't know if Earl Weaver is the greatest manager of all time, but he is close," said Indians President Gabe Paul. "He certainly is the best around now. He is fearless. He uses his 25 players better than [any manager] I have ever seen. He knows his statistics and he runs the game as well as anyone. And he knows the rules."

If you don't think so, just ask Reggie Jackson. To Weaver, a rule is something etched in stone like the Ten Commandments. "Don't fuck with my rules," is one of his favorite expressions.

Most don't.

"Weaver's style of managing is to show every player that he is not as good as he thinks he is, so he will go out and try to play better than he really thought he could," said Orioles catcher Rick Dempsey. "He can't be close to the players. He likes to sit back and crack the whip. The team works well for him. But he does scream an awful lot. He pushes and pushes and then backs off. No one likes it very much."

"Players are cautious about Earl," Orioles shortstop Mark Belanger once said. "There is no sense rocking the boat. He has been successful. He also has had great players."

The Orioles are probably baseball's real family. They are close and they enjoy each other's company after games and during the off-season. That is a rarity. But some players resent Weaver for the amount of publicity he receives. Furthermore, a few veterans have said that Earl, "Never taught me a thing." They explain that he receives all the credit, yet he has never knocked in a run in the majors. Also, he is seldom criticized when they lose.

"You have to remember this," says Orioles centerfielder Al Bumbry. "Earl does not ask for the attention. The writers come to him." Weaver himself has said that only one of his players ever liked him. That was Dean Chance, who played for Weaver in 1960 at Fox Cities.

Nevertheless, the Orioles call themselves, "the illegitimate sons of Earl Weaver." Stars Ken Singleton and Eddie Murray often charge each other with being "Earl's favorite son."

Orioles pitcher Steve Stone told *Time* magazine, "Earl tells you that he's the boss. Most managers don't have to tell you that all the time. It's a classic Napoleonic complex."

Because Weaver is five feet, seven inches tall, many have blamed his fire, his mouth and his drive to win every game and every argument on his size. It's the old adage about the little kid wanting to prove he can play with the big boys by starting fights and hurling insults.

Some feel this is the reason Earl makes statements like, "I could win 86 games with the [Toronto] Blue Jays." He said that in 1979, when Toronto played baseball like a bunch of Laplanders. If Weaver won 86 games with the Blue Jays, he would not only be a genius, he would be Moses.

When asked how he could compete with the Yankees and Steinbrenner's bottomless bank account, Earl says, "We'll out-administer them." The meaning is clear. Weaver believes that his team and its manager are the smartest in baseball.

"Look, I like to win," says Earl. "It doesn't matter if the game is cards, checkers or Monopoly. It would be the same if I were 6-foot-7 instead of 5-foot-7. I just wish the stupid people in the world would stop worrying about the little guys. A little guy is no different than anyone else."

That does not stop the Orioles from making cutting remarks about Earl's stature. In the middle of one of those infamous debates between Jim Palmer and Weaver, Palmer said, "Earl, I never saw you looking so tall." After becoming an Orioles coach, Frank Robinson was asked if he was a threat to Weaver's job. "Earl doesn't have to worry about me looking over his shoulder," said Robinson. "I can see over his head." Once a Japanese sumo wrestler came into the Orioles dressing room. Spotting Weaver, he immediately picked him up and held Earl above his head. "Drop him," yelled several Orioles between laughs.

Weaver is not fazed by these things. He appreciates a good line, even when he is the victim. Of course, he does not like being the target in a verbal shooting gallery. Then again, few have mouths capable of competing with Earl.

"Don't be fooled," says Milwaukee Brewers General Manager Harry Dalton. "Earl has a great mind. He would have been a success in almost any field. He has an engaging personality and I think he would have been a super businessman. He did very well in his various winter jobs. That guy is more than a good baseball man."

Earl's greatest asset is his intelligence," said former Orioles Minor League Director Jim McLaughlin, who hired Weaver for his first full-time professional managing position. "There are certain people in the world who were born to play ball. Take Boog Powell. He was big and strong, a natural power hitter. Now Earl can think, and that is why I believe he is a natural manager. If there are natural players, then there are natural managers."

McLaughlin seems to be correct. Weaver's record underlines the statement. So does the way he handled Reggie Jackson. Not only did he convince Jackson to wear a tie without creating a colossal power struggle—a la Billy Martin—he demonstrated to Reggie that he had something to learn about baseball. In one game, Jackson was on first base with Boog Powell at bat. Reggie stole second and thought he had made a brilliant play. Weaver bellowed at him. Jackson could not understand Weaver's unhappiness until he saw the pitcher intentionally walking Powell.

"You took the bat right out of Powell's hands," Earl told Jackson. "He hits homers. He wins games. There is nothing wrong with stealing, if you do it at the right time."

Jackson spent only one year under Earl and it was not easy.

"Reggie held out and reported to us a month into the season," recalled Weaver. "It took him another month to play himself into shape. Then, he started to hit until this game when Doc Ellis was throwing at our hitters. Reggie was mad. He yelled at Ellis, 'If you're gonna hit anyone, hit me.' In his next at bat, Ellis drilled Reggie in the jaw and that set him back another month. Still, Reggie had the best two months for me of anyone I have had."

"Earl Weaver is the best manager I ever played for," Jackson says today.

On one hand, there is Earl Weaver the genius and the egotist. On the flip side is Earl Weaver the man who works in his garden. He loves and respects his parents, not wanting to embarrass them. He won't be accused of corrupting youth by being photographed smoking a cigarette.

"My parents would yell at me when they heard I got thrown out of a game or into a fight with Palmer," said Weaver. "They would ask me why I wanted to hurt them by acting like a fool."

He worries about what his parents think of him. He is a good and loyal son to his mother. His father died in Weaver's arms during the winter of 1980–81.

Earl has a loose tongue, but he is tight with his money, despite his $150,000 salary. He saves Raleigh cigarette coupons and owns a modest winter home in Miami and a summer place in the casual Baltimore suburb of Perry Hall. For him, a splurge is his Cadillac and his swimming pool. He is a man who puts salt in his beer and frets about the inflation rate, which makes retirement a more difficult proposition. He often negotiates his contracts in the newspapers, dropping hints that he might look elsewhere if his demands are not met. He was a depression child and has a trace of that era's insecurity in his character.

He is Earl Weaver the manager. Earl Weaver the hothead who does advertisements for air conditioners. He is Earl Weaver the father, son, and husband, winner and resident genius. To Orioles fans, he is the Earl of Baltimore. All of this and more make up Earl Weaver the man.

2

The Busher

The year was 1979 and the Orioles had just completed a three-game series in Kansas City.

Kansas City. The name causes Earl Weaver to cringe. Royals Stadium is the Orioles' lions' den. Entering the 1979 season, the Birds had a 16–25 record in Kansas City. A week before Baltimore was to play there, Weaver would begin moaning to the writers.

"Kansas City," he'd say. "Do you know what happened there last year? John Wathan hit a ground ball over first base. It got by [Eddie] Murray and started rolling. Wathan is a catcher. Anyhow, the ball keeps rolling on that damn artificial turf and goes into the right-field corner. Kenny [Singleton] is playing right field and he goes after it. Kenny tries hard, but he's no track star. He gets behind the ball and starts chasing it. It rolls into the corner and hugs the wall. Kenny is running after it and Wathan is running around the bases. By the time Kenny gets to it, Wathan has scored. Can you fucking believe that? A catcher hit a ground ball home run. It could only happen in Kansas City."

Weaver is Alfred Hitchcock when it comes to Kansas City tales. He has a wealth of them and they all end with the Orioles being annihilated in some gory fashion.

9

"I don't know how many times that George Brett has beat us here," said Weaver. "I know the guy is great, but he is fucking Superman when we play him. He doesn't just hit the ball out of the park against us, he hits it into the damn waterfalls about nine miles away in right field. Our pitchers get stupid when they see him. So stupid sometimes they throw him fastballs. Fastballs to Brett. Terrific!"

Earl's major problem with Kansas City is his famed statistics. They are a horror story. Weaver worships and trusts numbers. Better than any other manager, he can assimilate tons of numerical material and translate it into human terms. For years, he has made the stats work for the Birds. They tell him what pinch hitter to use or who to put into the lineup.

In that respect, the Orioles are a cold, calculating team. They make few mistakes and wear the opposition down as Weaver shuffles players in and out of the lineup like a general deploying reinforcements. You can beat the Birds in the sprints—which is often what games on the Kansas City turf become—but over the course of 162 games they will be at or near the top, always pushing hard in the end. They are the marathon runner whose final mile is faster than his first, and that is why Weaver has the best September record of any manager in baseball.

Yes, the Orioles are a slot machine team. You throw in your quarters and you may win a pot here and a few dollars there. But when it is over, you will come up short because they have the odds on their side. Weaver knows this. His numbers tell him so.

But when it came to playing in Kansas City, the stats said the Birds were in for a Royal beating.

"Look at these," he said as the Orioles prepared to face the Royals for the first time in 1979. "Brett is hitting .426 against us. Darrell Porter .388. Wathan .410. It goes on and on. They all hit us."

The unmentionable part of this lament was that Earl may be a genius, but he would have required the wisdom of Solomon to handle Kansas City. During the three preceding years, the Orioles were pleased to leave town with one win in a series.

"There is something about this place," Orioles shortstop Mark Belanger once said. "Bad things just happen to us here."

It would be different in the pennant-winning season of 1979. The Orioles split six games in KC and even won two of three games in a series. Their first series victory on the Royals' carpet since 1974. And that is where we pick up this story.

The date was July 29. The Birds had been shot down by the Royals the night before. That tied the series at 1—1, but what made it worse was that Baltimore outfielder Gary Roenicke was smashed in the back by a fastball. He spent Saturday night in the hospital with a yellowish—blue bruise the size of a basketball blossoming on his lower back. On Sunday morning Weaver was obsessed with having Roenicke start.

"We gotta get him in there," said Weaver. "I don't care if he is hurting, so long as he can swing the bat. Paul Splittorff is starting for them. Roenicke has great stats against Splittorff. He crushes him."

"Saturday was not a great night for me," recalled Roenicke. "After I was hit I spent two hours in the clubhouse with ice on my back. Then I went to the hospital and wasted a bunch of time there. They sent me back to my hotel room early in the morning and I couldn't sleep. I couldn't even lift my left arm. I never thought I could play."

Earl kept having Orioles trainer Ralph Salvon call Roenicke's room to check on his condition. At first, Roenicke was not going to show up for the game. He was miserable and his back throbbed. But he came, anyhow, and saw his name in the lineup. He did some exercises and running. Soon, he said he was loose enough to play.

In his first at bat, he homered against Splittorff, and the Orioles were on their way to a 6—4 win. After the game Weaver wore a smug smile.

"I knew that Roenicke was hurting so I sent two of my friends to see him," said Weaver. "Their names are Dr. Long Ball and his assistant, Dr. Three Hit. They did their job."

As the Orioles trudged onto the bus to the Kansas City

airport following the game, Earl was still discussing Dr. Long Ball's visit to Roenicke. "I don't know if it was a miracle, but somebody cured his bat because it has been pretty sick lately."

Naturally, the Orioles were in a joyous mood as they departed. Weaver took note that they had a woman bus driver. He spoke to her for a few minutes, and then told all those sitting around him, "She's all right, she's an Elmira girl." Weaver met his second wife, Marianna, in Elmira, New York. It is an hour ride from Royals Stadium to the airport. After 40 minutes, Weaver noticed that something was wrong.

"I just saw a sign that said St. Joseph," said Weaver. "That ain't right. We're going in the opposite direction. I guess this is what happens when you leave the driving to a pair of tits."

A line like that is great stuff in a baseball environment. Weaver did grow a bit red when he realized that his "Elmira girl" behind the wheel might have overheard him. He apologized, but she was oblivious to everything around her. Eventually, she found the airport, but the sign to St. Joseph had put Earl in a nostalgic state of mind.

"You know, I began my pro career in St. Joe's," he told the writers in the front of the bus.

Earl Sidney Weaver, Jr. was born August 14, 1930 in St. Louis. His father was a dry cleaner and a baseball fan, not necessarily in that order. Earl's passion for the game came very early.

"My dad used to clean the uniforms for the St. Louis Cardinals and Browns," said Weaver. "It was my job to deliver them and get them from the park. That was a thrill. I would walk into the locker rooms and see the ballplayers. My eyes would grow really wide. I was a Cardinals fan. I loved the old Gas House Gang."

In retrospect, Weaver would have been the ideal manager for the Cardinals of the 1930s. They were his kind of team—a group of shrewd ass kickers. Given the choice between destroying a pivoting second baseman with a slide or stepping aside, they went in low and hard. Their third baseman was Pepper Martin, a man who preferred to play ground balls off his chest before throwing to first base. There was Joe Medwick, who was blasted with fruit and bottles by the Detroit fans in the 1934 World Series for decking a third baseman with a spikes-high slide. Medwick had to leave the game for his own safety, but it hardly mattered because the Gas House Gang was on its way to a Series triumph. There was also Enos Slaughter, who never learned that he could not catch a fly ball hit over a wall. He kept trying to run through walls to catch them. Finally, there was Dizzy Dean, a pitcher whose boasting and penchant for butchering the English language surpassed his pitching. Weaver seems to be carrying Dean's grammatical torch. His sentences are held up by dangling modifiers and mixed metaphors with a healthy sprinkling of obscenities and ain'ts and other solecisms.

Yes, the Cardinals were exciting and they were mean.

Weaver loved their style. He copied them and longed to be one of them. He still fondly speaks of those great St. Louis teams, although he does not tolerate one of their favorite tactics—the beanball. Earl will not allow his pitchers to throw at hitters. Pitching inside is one thing, but throwing behind a batter (so that he will back into the delivery) is forbidden.

Weaver was small, but his mouth and wit were large. He was a zealot on the diamond, performing with a vengeance. He played in the Khoury Leagues and on two city championship clubs at Beaumont High. His teammates were former Senators' star Roy Sievers and Giants' infielder Bobby Hofman, who fondly recalls those times, often speaking of a home run he swatted at 15 during an amateur game in Sportsman's Park.

"We had a great team at Beaumont," said Hofman. "There were six or seven guys who signed pro contracts. I don't know if that is a record or anything, but it is pretty impressive.

"I was a senior when Earl made the team as a freshman. Since I had been playing second base for three years, Earl played third that year. Then he took over for me after I graduated. He started as a freshman and probably hit over .400. We had an outstanding coach, a man named Ray Elliot. He used to have us working out in the gym during the winter, hitting tennis balls and things like that. Back then, that was revolutionary. Some people thought he was crazy with all the drills he put us through inside. But he was ahead of his time and he was part of the reason we won city titles."

Hofman says that Weaver was an above-average student and not nearly as combative as one would expect.

"He came from a nice home and a good family," recalled Hofman. "Once, we went on a double date. Earl didn't like the way that ended up because I dumped his girlfriend and him and took off with the car and my girl."

After graduation Hofman was signed by the New York Giants. He was in the majors by 1949, a year after Weaver began his pro career. Hofman was a coach for the Cleveland Indians and Oakland A's. He is now the New York Yankees Director of Scouting.

"Earl always did know the game," said Hofman. "In high school, it was impossible to predict that he would become a great manager. Who could tell? But I was not surprised that he signed a contract. He worked hard, was a good fielder, and he had some pop with his bat."

"You know, Earl was something," said Earl Weaver, Sr. "He was 17 when he signed his first pro pact. I managed him for four years on the sandlots and we finished in first place four times."

During the past decade Earl Weaver, Sr. would spend a month of each summer with his son in Baltimore. The two men would leave at 3 P.M. for Memorial Stadium. Earl would respectfully introduce his father to the writers who stopped in his office before and after games. Earl Weaver, Sr. said little. He seemed mesmerized by the fact that all these newspapermen stood with pens and notebooks poised, ready to record his son's every word. On those rare occasions when he did speak, it was to inform some scribe that his son was 17 when he signed or that he managed Earl's summer teams to four straight pennants.

The message was clear—managing and winning were a part of the family.

"I used to love it at old Sportsman's Park," said Weaver. "Between the Cardinals and old Browns, I went to 100 games a summer. And I used to watch the games closely. I would be there, mulling over and second guessing the moves of [Cardinals' manager] Billy Southworth. Hell, I was 12 years old and I thought I knew more than he did."

"Earl was an intelligent ballplayer," said former St. Louis Browns Minor League Director Jim McLaughlin. "I scouted him several times in high school. I liked his desire. He had a willingness to apply himself to studying the game even at that early age. That was the thing that stuck with me about Earl. I'll never forget how hungry he was to succeed and learn all he could. He was not very big, maybe 5-7 and 160 pounds. While his size worked against him, it was not the only reason he was not a top prospect. He did not have a real good arm or any speed. He handled second base very well and hit okay. But it was his motivation that made him a candidate to sign. We thought he could be an Eddie Stanky-type player, the kind of guy who beats you more with his guts than his ability. But when we sat down and realistically evaluated him, we felt he would be a Class AAA player at best, just a little short of the majors."

McLaughlin's analysis of Weaver would be correct on two counts. First, he never did break into Class AAA. Second, he did possess a tremendous aptitude for the game.

The Cardinals also had their eye on Weaver. Earl talked to both teams after graduating from Beaumont. The Browns were cautious. They spent a large part of their meeting telling Weaver the limit of his talents. It was the old tactic of running down a kid's ability so that he would be grateful to sign a contract without a bonus.

The Cardinals were a different story. They were wealthy, although never overly generous with their minor league personnel. They had 13 farm clubs at that time and Weaver likes to recall that they "were signing anybody who could walk and breathe." Because Weaver could do more than that, Cardinals Minor League Director Walter Shannon offered him a $1,000 bonus. But it was Shannon's salesmanship more than the money that made Earl want to be a Cardinal.

"Walter Shannon walked with me to Sportsman's Park and pointed to second base," said Weaver. "He told me that I would be out there in a couple of seasons. I about broke his wrist shaking his hand on the deal and I couldn't wait to get the pen to sign the contract."

Ironically, the Browns later moved to Baltimore and became the Orioles. McLaughlin gave Earl his first full-time managing job, largely because of the impression he had made at 17. Eventually, Shannon became a Baltimore scout. Thus all three men became members of the Orioles' fine farm department.

The St. Louis Cardinals sent their minor leaguers to spring training in Albany, Georgia. Now, those players spend their spring in the same town as the major league club. But few teams have more than 150 players in camp. In 1948, most clubs had more than 400 players vying for spots in the minor leagues.

"With the Cardinals, it was even worse," said Hofman. "They had working agreements with 13 farm clubs and that meant they always had 500–600 guys in training camp."

"Back then you could get an invitation to spring training if you could write a convincing letter to a team's farm department," said Orioles General Manager Hank Peters, whose first baseball job was serving as McLaughlin's assistant with the Browns.

Numbers dictated that minor leaguers have their own training site. Usually, it was someplace like Albany where the weather was warm and the rent cheap. Albany, Georgia would never be confused with St. Petersburg, Miami, or Ft. Lauderdale, Florida, but that was fine with the Cardinals. This was not a spring vacation. Weaver left St. Louis with Harley Beavers, a friend who was also signed by the Cardinals. The train ride to Albany took more than 24 hours, and they arrived at midnight.

"When we got off the train, someone who worked at the station asked us if we were ballplayers," recalled Weaver. "They sent us on a bus to the public square. From there, we were sent to various private homes where we would stay."

Earl was ordered to report to the local YMCA at 10 A.M. He was assigned to the Cards' Class B Lynchburg club and given $1.25, his meal money for the day.

Weaver tells the rest of the story as reported by *Baltimore Evening Sun* baseball writer Phil Jackman.

"That first day was something," Weaver told Jackman. "All 13 of the Cards' farm clubs were in Albany and each one had four second basemen. So what does that come to, 52? You can't imagine how bad I felt when I walked into the clubhouse and saw all those guys. And it got worse when I walked onto the field. Actually, there was no field. All you could see was bodies from home plate to the center field fence. I was 17 then and I tell you, if I would have known how to get home, I wouldn't be managing today. I felt like crying. Then I thought back to my going away party and the shaving bag my parents gave me. I said to myself, 'what the heck, let's go out there and see what we can do.' They ran you through this system to get uniforms just like in the army. Who cares if it fits? Put it on. And they threw the stuff at you. My first number was 500 and something."

There were eight second basemen with the Lynchburg club. Infield drills were like tightrope walks. Each player handled every ground ball as if it were a life-and-death struggle. In many ways, it was. If you missed two in a row, you were sent to a lower level or released. Naturally, each player prayed that the other second basemen's hands would suddenly turn to stone. Despite much shaking and a stomach in need of a massive dose of Alka Seltzer, Weaver didn't miss. But that did not stop him from being cut twice. Three times and he was out.

Until the 1960s, the minors were like spider webs, extending in many directions from the cores which were the major league teams. Class AAA was the highest level followed by AA, A, B, C, and D. Weaver started at Class B, then was bounced to C, and finally D.

"You know how they used to cut guys?" asked Weaver. "Somebody would get up early in the morning with a list in his hand and start reading off numbers. If your number came up, you were told to go to a certain place and that was the last you ever saw of that player. He was gone. They got their bus tickets home."

Weaver survived the final purge and was dispatched to West Frankfort, Illinois. He was starting at the bottom, No. 13 of the Cards' 13 teams.

Today it is hard to imagine West Frankfort with a professional baseball team. It is a town of 8,900 people in southern Illinois, about 75 miles southeast of St. Louis. It is divided by Highway 37, but the traffic was reduced when Interstate 57 was built a few miles away.

Earl Weaver could not have cared less about the history or location of West Frankfort. To him it meant that he was now a professional ballplayer and West Frankfort would be a place he would one day recall as the starting point of an illustrious major league career. In some respects, he was correct. But in the tremendous future he envisioned, he would be a player.

After his first minor league at bat, he had no doubt that he would be starting for the Cards at Sportsman's Park, just as Walter Shannon had predicted.

"I homered my first time up," said Weaver. "That was a great feeling. I thought, major leagues, here I come. This is easy."

After he had trotted around the bases, Weaver's teammates pointed him toward the outfield fence. There he saw a hole through which the West Frankfort fans were throwing money onto the field. It was their way of backing the team. Earl sprinted to the fence and stuffed his pockets with the cash.

Ah, life in the minors. Weaver would learn to love and to hate it. Most players are clobbered with the same conflicting emotions. Once they retire, all they remember are the games, the fans, the teenage girls who hung around the clubhouse after the games, and suppers of hot dogs and soft drinks purchased at the concession stands. Even the brutal bus rides, the cramped, sweaty dressing rooms with leaky showers, and the perpetually running toilets seem tolerable in retrospect.

At West Frankfort Weaver was listed as 17 years old, 5-foot-6 ½ inches and 155 pounds. Like the rest of his teammates, he would learn of the dead hours before and after a game in the hamlets of the Illinois State League. Except for truck stops, all restaurants were closed when the games were over. Not that it mattered because $1.50 meal money and $200 a month salaries bought little more than subsistence food, toothpaste, and underwear. If the games were over quickly, the players would sneak into a theater and catch the last few minutes of a movie. Most stayed up until the early morning hours and did not awaken much before noon.

The time before the game was the longest. That period from noon to 5 P.M. often felt like a month. The players would walk up and down the main street, stopping in the drug store for coffee or Coke at the soda fountain. They examined the magazine racks daily, they roamed the aisles at the dime and department stores. They saw everything 1,000 times, but they kept looking for something new. It also gave them a chance to watch the female clerks and young housewives who frequented the stores.

They talked of baseball and broads. A player with a car was someone special. His teammates treaded carefully around him, hoping he would take them for a ride, to a drive-in, anywhere. If a ballplayer had a car, he was more likely to have a girl in town. "Local meat," they sometimes called these women. As this was the first time away from home for most players, having a high-school girl with braces or a slightly wrinkled divorcee as a companion was a treat. It gave you someone to share the trials of the day with besides your teammates. After all, every player had his own list of grievances against the manager, umpires, farm department, and other players. But a local girl offered a sympathetic ear. In most cases, she was convinced that your problems were unique since this usually was her first contact with professional baseball. If the mood was right, the player's story pitiful or gloriously dreamy, she would offer a hug and a kiss. Sometimes, these women even ended up as player's wives. Frequently, they were mother figures for a summer.

But most players were not blessed with the company of a waitress, clerk, or high-school girl. They were on their own. Their girlfriends were back in Detroit, Boston, Paducah, or St. Louis. Many wrote them daily love letters, composed while staring at the girl's picture. Most ballplayers lived in boarding houses and mail from home was an important and solemn occasion. Letters sometimes were passed around among friends. Players shared tales of late-night backseat liaisons that happened, supposedly happened, or were to happen once the season concluded. It was something to do besides walk the streets and haunt the stores.

Another big event was obtaining the latest copy of the *Sporting News*. The players immediately turned to the back for the minor league statistics. They checked the performance of the athletes at their positions who were in the classification ahead of them. For example, players at Class D West Frankfort studied the numbers of those with the Cardinals' Class C Duluth club. If the Class C player at your position was having a poor season, usually you ranted and bitched about the ignorance of the Cardinals for keeping you at West Frankfort when you clearly should be in Duluth. Hell, all you have to do is look at the *Sporting News*.

Weaver was content in West Frankfort. Naturally he wanted to advance, but he was pleased with the events of his first season. Not bad for a kid 17, he thought.

Earl Weaver also had a girl in St. Louis and he would marry her once he turned 18. But first he had to finish his maiden season, and he did it with style.

He hit only one more home run after that first at bat. In fact, he had only 38 in nine full seasons, but he fondly recalls every one. He batted .268, scored 96 runs, and drove in 48. Those statistics are commendable, but hardly the stuff of a league's Most Valuable Player. Nevertheless, Weaver received that award.

Part of the reason was that West Frankfort won the Illinois State League championship and Earl was the top fielding second baseman. That is only a partial explanation. Weaver not only played well, he played hard. He was like a member of his beloved Gas House Gang. He knocked opposing second basemen into the dirt with vicious slides. He always seemed to know where to throw the ball and what would happen next. He made a lot of noise, constantly reminding his teammates of the number of outs. Fans always are drawn to players with those traits, and they embraced Earl. He was a guy who actually liked those drills in which a runner is sent like a kamikaze to roll into a pivoting second baseman. Members of the Cardinals' minor league organization say that most athletes shunned the exercise. It left them sore, bruised, and often with scrapes and cuts which then became infected with the infield dust. More than anything, it was this spirit that made Weaver MVP.

As Earl prepared to leave for spring training in 1949, he was secure. He had had a fine rookie season and was the MVP, even if it was in Class D. The Cardinals told him to report to Sportsman's Park where he would catch a bus to Albany, Georgia. When he arrived, he was stunned. There were more than 70 players waiting for the same bus. They all were from St. Louis and they all had been signed by the Cardinals.

The scene in Albany was pretty much the same. There seemed to be a million guys, and a couple thousand of them claiming to be second basemen. That was how it looked to Earl. He spent the 1949 season with the Cards' Class C team in St. Joseph, Missouri. When the year was over, Weaver again was named MVP. This time, he was tops in the Western Association as his team rolled to a pennant with a 96–48 record. The incredible aspect of Weaver's performance that year was that he had 101 runs batted in, but only two home runs and a .282 batting average.

"I don't think there were too many guys in baseball history with two homers who drove in more than 100 runs," says Earl. "That year, I doubt that I ever failed to drive a runner in from third with less than two outs. I had one of those seasons where you always come through in the clutch."

Weaver continued to cut his way through the jungle which was the Cardinal farm system. He spent 1950 in the Class B Carolina League with Winston–Salem. He batted .260 with 3 HR and 60 RBI, while committing 16 errors, the lowest total among Carolina League second basemen. Winston–Salem went 106–47 to give Weaver his third title in as many pro seasons. He was promoted to Class AA Houston at the start of 1951, but after hitting .233 in 43 at bats, he was sent to Class A Omaha. There, he went on to become the Western League MVP thanks to his adroit fielding, a .279 batting average and 52 RBI.

"I remember playing against Earl in the Minors," says Indians Manager Dave Garcia. "He was always getting into fights. I had been playing for a while and since we both were from St. Louis, I thought I'd talk to him about it. One day I got to second base and I said, 'Earl, you've got to stop this fighting.' He looked over from his position and said, 'Ah, fuck you.' "

Most of all, it was this competitiveness, his verve which put him above his peers. It also earned him an invitation to train with St. Louis in St. Petersburg, Florida.

The Cardinals' incumbent second baseman was Red Schoendienst. He had held the job since 1945. In 1951, he batted .289 and was in the midst of a bitter contract dispute with the Cardinals. He sat out much of spring training and second base was held by 21-year-old Earl Weaver. Earl was impressive defensively and batted .280. Then Schoendienst came to terms with the Cards and Weaver was demoted to Houston.

Earl had no idea that this would be his only trial with a major league team. The next time he attended a big league training camp would be 1969, his first full year as manager of the Baltimore Orioles, and he still talks of that spring with the Cardinals. It was his chance to play next to his idols. Eddie Stanky—the player to whom Weaver was most often compared—was the manager. Earl dressed in the same clubhouse with Stan Musial and Enos Slaughter, two players he had gaped at when delivering uniforms to Sportsman's Park from his father's cleaning store years before.

Weaver did not take his demotion to Houston well. For the first time in his career he pouted. This attitude carried over to his play. After half a season at Houston he was batting .219 and this was the first time in his pro career that he was not on a pennant winner. The St. Louis front office was not pleased with Earl's batting average, and they wondered what had changed his usually aggressive attitude.

They decided to ship him further down, back to Class A Omaha. Naturally, that didn't thrill Earl. And when he learned that the Cards also wanted to cut his salary from $600 to $400 a month, he was furious. He yelled and called on the gods to right this injustice. Then he jumped in his car and drove home to St. Louis. His career was slipping away. Being cut was bad enough, but a slap in the wallet was too much. His holdout lasted one day, as the Cards relented and told him it had all been a misunderstanding. Why, of course he would still make $600 a month at Omaha.

This was the first contract war Earl would win, but not the last. Weaver spent the 1952–53 baseball seasons in Omaha, where he batted .278 and .243 and discovered that the Cardinals no longer considered him a prospect. His manager there was Gene Kissell, an intense man who reached the point where he could not watch a game in the late, crucial innings. During a tight situation, he would say to someone around him, "Broadcast the game to me, I can't look."

"Earl does things like that with the Orioles," says former Baltimore star Brooks Robinson. Sometimes, he goes down the dugout runway where he can't see the game and then waits for the crowd noise to let him know what happened."

In 1955, Weaver was sold to the Pirates. He had a solid season at Class AA New Orleans, batting .278 with a career high 6 HR and 59 RBI.

"That was a good season, but I passed through waivers (where he could have been claimed by any team for $25,000) the next year," says Weaver. "So I figured that I wasn't good enough, or at least nobody thought I was."

3

The Climb to Baltimore

Once again we are on the Orioles' team bus. It is the spring of 1979. The Birds have finished a game in Bradenton, Florida, just outside of Tampa. In front of them is a six-hour ride back to their spring training home in Miami.

This has been a rough trip for the Orioles and Weaver. It began with a 15-inning, 2–1 loss to Montreal in Daytona Beach. Most exhibitions are called off if a winner does not emerge in something like 12 innings. It is considered pointless to keep on playing when the game doesn't count.

"I guess we could have had a gentleman's agreement to quit," says Weaver. "But [Montreal Manager] Dick Williams is no gentleman and neither am I."

Baltimore General Manager Hank Peters says something to Weaver about the Orioles' failure to bunt.

"Hank, what good is bunting when you can't hit," says Weaver shaking his head. He says it is "almost always a stupid move," and it is the last thing he wanted to hear—even from his boss—after this absurd spring contest. Earl then pounds the clubhouse door with his fist.

So the Orioles stumble aboard the bus, travel to Bradenton and play the Pirates. That produces another loss, which does not leave them in the best frame of mind as they prepare to depart for Miami.

There is something about ballplayers and buses. A closeness, yet a repulsion. The bus is the symbol of their stay in the minors, the $6,000 salary and $8 a day meal money. You pay your dues on the Greyhound, and once you reach the majors it is something you long to forget.

In the minors the bus is where you eat, sleep, drink, talk, write letters, change clothes, and go to the bathroom. It is your home away from home, especially if you play in the Southern or Texas leagues. There, the average trip is six hours, and 10–12 hour treks are not unusual. You pile on after a game and stay on as the sun comes up, arriving at your hotel in mid-morning. Often it is agonizingly hot and those are the times when the air conditioner is broken and when even breathing creates beads of sweat and any movement causes a veritable flood of perspiration. Some players sleep on the floor, others in the overhead luggage compartments. Few can sleep in the seats, where there always seems to be a handle sticking in your side, adding to the aches that come from having your body contorted like a pretzel to keep your feet off the floor.

Weaver spent 20 years on the bus. All of the Orioles have tasted the life, and they thought about those days on the ride from Bradenton to Miami. Weaver argued with coaches Jim Frey, Cal Ripken, and Elrod Hendricks about who had taken the longest and most miserable bus trip. Hendricks launched into a lengthy account of a 22-hour ride he once took through the heart of Mexico down snake-like roads built for burros.

Someone recalled several stories of Weaver on buses. After one tough loss to Texas, Weaver had screamed at a driver who was struggling with a clutch.

"For Christsake, step on the damn thing," Weaver told the driver.

"Listen, you just manage your goddamn team and I'll take care of the bus," said the driver, sending Earl into one of the few periods of silence in his life.

"Earl's secret wish is to be a bus driver," Orioles Pitching Coach Ray Miller once said. Weaver obviously feels he knows more about the vehicles than the drivers. After all, he has been riding them longer than most of the men behind the wheel.

As the Orioles made their way back to Miami they went down "Alligator Alley." Ray Miller along with Orioles players Eddie Murray and Dave Skaggs began watching for gators. Soon they were counting the reptiles, competing to see who could spot the most. In the back seat, Al Bumbry was hooking a rug while most of the other Orioles played cards, drank beer, or stared out the windows. The bus stopped at a Burger King, where the players had supper. Instead of complaining they seemed to enjoy downing the double cheeseburgers, greasy fries, and shakes.

Weaver spent the trip in the right front seat. No one was next to him. There never is. That is the manager's spot, and Weaver looks like he belongs right up front. He has that quality. It is something Jim McLaughlin saw in him as a 17-year-old high-school player, and it has saved his career in baseball.

By 1956, Weaver knew he was in trouble. He had not been at a big league spring training camp in four years. He was earning $800 a month. His new team, the Pirates, had no plans for him. He began that season at Class AA New Orleans. Then he was sold to Class A Montgomery and dealt later in the year to Knoxville.

Knoxville was a Class A independent farm club in the Sally League. Independent meant that it was not connected with any major league organization. Its players often were castoffs like Weaver, or young athletes no one else was willing to sign. The team was called the Smokies, and there was little fire about them. They were the classic example of an overmatched, "dead-ass" team. They lost frequently and looked bad doing it. One of the few bright spots was Weaver, who was back to his usual hustling self. He was the team captain and one of the few players who cared about winning.

As the Smokies continued to smolder, the owners decided that it was time for a managerial change. Dick Bartell was axed.

Earl Weaver, a 26-year-old second baseman, was called in for a meeting.

"We want you to take over the team," the owners told him.

Weaver said he wasn't interested. He empathized with the recently fired manager. Besides, he knew that becoming a manager would be the end for him as a player. You don't make the majors as a player by running the Knoxville Smokies. "When they ask you to manage, they are saying that you no longer are a major league prospect," explained Weaver. "When that happened to me, it broke my heart."

Even though he had bounced between three minor league teams in 1956, even though he had not been to a big league spring training since 1952, and even though his beloved Cardinals had cast him aside like a shoe they had outgrown, Weaver still clung to the dream. He was going to make it, prove the scouts wrong and turn Walter Shannon into a prophet. He would still play second base for someone at Sportsman's Park. After all, he was a five-time All-Star and had won four MVP awards.

By being asked to run the Smokies Earl was staring straight at the end of his playing career. For two weeks he ignored the situation. He made out the lineup and continued to handle the second base chores. Periodically, the front office brought up the subject of managing. They also offered him a $200 a month raise. That was when Earl finally agreed.

Under Weaver the Smokies went 10–24. They were the pits of the Sally League.

"I was then Assistant Farm Director with the Orioles in 1956," says Harry Dalton, now the Brewers General Manager. "I was in Knoxville, talking to them about joining the Orioles' farm system in 1957. That same day they fired their manager and put Earl in charge. They were a terrible, terrible team. But Earl had lots of enthusiasm and worked hard. The fans loved him. I think he knew that he was not big league material as a player back then, and he started acting like the manager right from the beginning."

When the St. Louis Browns moved to Baltimore in 1954, Minor League Director Jim McLaughlin did not forget about Weaver. He was happy to learn that Earl had been named the Smokies' manager and he sent Orioles Scout Jim Russo to watch him in action.

"I was impressed right away by Weaver," said Russo. "Jim McLaughlin had an interest in him as a manager and wanted to hear what I thought. Earl was very wrapped up in the game. He seemed to have the talent to ignite players and create excitement even in a dead atmosphere like Knoxville was that season. Earl was still playing second base then. He had the good glove, but he was not much of a hitter and had little speed."

Some claim Red Schoendienst was the reason Weaver never played in the majors. Schoendienst had a lifetime .289 major league batting average (compared with .267 for Weaver in the bushes). Schoendienst was a 10-time All-Star and an institution at second in St. Louis. He is still a part of the Cardinals, now serving as a coach. Viewing the situation in the cold, objective manner that would later be his trademark, Weaver refuses to buy the assertion that he was with the wrong team at the wrong time.

"I could have made it as a utility man if I had had a better arm. Or if I had been blessed with Al Bumbry's speed. I guess I did not have quite enough."

Earl returned home to St. Louis for the winters of 1956–57. He was a family man with three children. In the summers he played baseball, and that was the key word. For $4,000 a year it was hard to call baseball a profession. Minor leaguers are paid according to how they play, not work. They must find gainful employment during the winter to pay the bills.

In his first pro season, 1948, Weaver had made only $300 a month during the season. He spent the next two winters as a warehouseman. In 1950, he was hired by the city of St. Louis to install, service, and empty parking meters. He also was a tax collector. Later he was a stone mason's helper and toiled 15 stories above the ground. He discovered that he was not suited for work in the upper atmosphere when he dropped a $400 piece of polished granite.

"A friend got me the job in construction in 1953," recalled Weaver. "It paid more money so I took it. I remember my first day of work. They told me to move this huge pile of sand across the yard. I busted my ass and got the job done by noon. I went to the boss and said I was finished. He said that the work was supposed to take me two days. He sent me home and told me to stay there the next day. All I got paid for was three hours."

Nor did he fare much better as a hod carrier.

"There were a bunch of us who carried bricks up a ladder on our backs," said Weaver. "The first time I was at the front, and I dropped my load on the other guys. After that they put me at the back of the line. They thought I was going to kill someone, although I didn't screw up any more loads."

All these jobs were stopgaps, fillers for a man with a mission. But the events of 1956 convinced Earl that it was time to get serious. The mission was aborted, and Weaver went to the Liberty Loan Company and took the test required of all potential employees.

"I scored the highest they ever had," said Weaver. "Well, I don't know for a fact that it was the highest, but it was damn good. They usually started you at $300 a month, but they gave me $400 and said I would get an office in two years. They had big plans for me."

Perhaps it was the native instinct and intelligence Jim McLaughlin spoke of, or Earl's willingness to plunge whole-heartedly into whatever endeavor he attempted. The bottom line, as they say in the loan business, was that Earl Weaver was a veritable genius when it came to deciding who was a good risk to repay a Liberty Loan. He treated the money as if it were his own, perhaps prizing it even more. He judged every customer carefully.

"Between my blue collar jobs and minor league baseball, I have been with every kind of person. I know people. All types. I have heard all the sob stories about the checks being in the mail or waiting just one more week until pay day. Listen, I could look into people's eyes and see if they would pay. I enjoyed the work, checking references and all that. I was strongly considering stay- ing with Liberty and forgetting baseball. When I told them I was going back, they begged me to stick with them."

Weaver insists that he never closed a bad loan for Liberty. It was this judgment of character, combined with his knowledge of baseball, that made him an attractive candidate to manage a minor league team. That was the conclusion of Jim Russo, Harry Dalton, and McLaughlin. So, McLaughlin offered him a chance to manage the Orioles Class D squad in Fitzgerald, Georgia. Although Weaver could see himself as a lifer with Liberty Loan, he leaped at the opportunity to call the shots in Fitzgerald for $3,500 a year. That came to $700 a month, $100 less than he had earned as a player.

In the spring of 1957, the Orioles sent their minor leaguers to train at Thomasville, Georgia. Like Albany, it was an armpit Georgia town with few distractions for those dedicating themselves to a clean life and a ticket to the majors, a family town on which 250 ballplayers descended every spring. The locals were overwhelmed by their numbers and at times were baffled by their behavior. For the players, they were deeply bored once they left the diamond.

Earl Weaver recalls the mob scene of his first day of spring training at Thomasville. He knew what it felt like to have a number like 571 and to look over your shoulder during an infield drill and see seven guys standing in line, waiting for a chance to take your job. Now, he was on the other end. It was his turn to watch eight second basemen and pick out the ones who could play. That was bad, but hardly the worst part.

As a player, Earl had never been cut. He was demoted, traded, sold and herded about like a steer in a stockyard, but he had never faced the axe. He had been able to step out of line before the slaughter. It is one thing to have someone tell you that you won't be playing in St. Louis this year, we are sending you to Omaha. It is quite another to be told that you can forget Omaha and baseball, too. Here's your bus ticket home.

While the Orioles had only half the number of minor leaguers as the Cardinals, it still was an absurd system. After 7–10 days of camp, names of players were posted.

"They were told to report to the manager," said Weaver. "It was the same as the death list."

But this time the manager was Earl, and it was now his role to end the dreams. The decision of who stayed and who talked to the manager was made at night following each practice. Players were evaluated and rated on hitting, fielding, speed, arm strength, and attitude. Each of the minor league managers, farm department brass, and scouts would grade every player on a numerical scale in each facet of the game. If a player's overall score was low, everyone in the room was asked if the athlete should be released.

If anyone wanted him retained he was kept. If there were no objections, his name appeared on the "death" list, and Weaver, like other Class D managers, would have to meet with the players.

"You know what they are thinking when they walk into the office," said Weaver. "They all were given a party and a shaving kit when they left home. Everybody said 'Okay kid, we'll see you in the majors in four years.' But you have to call them and say that it is the consensus of the staff that we have to let you go. Some of them cry, others get mad, a few go crazy. One pulled a knife on me. But they all want to know one thing.

"They look at you and ask, 'Skipper, what do you think?' You have to look them in the eye and say, 'You can't make my team.' If you say it mean enough, then maybe you can save them a few years of learning what you saw in a day. The bottom line is that they aren't good enough to play in the majors, just like I didn't have enough talent. If you don't have the ability, no amount of hard work or desire can do it for you.

"On that first day with these kids you learn that you are always going to have to be a rotten son of a bitch. In my case, a little, rotten son of a bitch. That's the way it is. To keep your job, you fire others or you bench them or get rid of them. That is why you can't get too close to any of them."

Earl often says that it did not bother him to give a player the worst news of his life. He also says that he sometimes told players in Thomasville that they could go to the Cardinals' camp in Albany and try again with another organization. During his years as a minor league manager, Weaver released only one player who later made it to the majors. He was Fred Whitfield, a first baseman who labored for a few summers with Cleveland. Only one such mistake in 11 years of minor league managing is a spectacular record.

"It is just part of the job," he said. "It is not personal. It is another part of baseball judgment. But sometimes you get tired of hurting people. You want to be a good guy and have everybody like you, but you can't."

"I said before that Earl was a natural manager," said Jim McLaughlin. "You could tell by the way he handled himself in our spring meetings. He was assertive and strong in his opinions about players, but he didn't dominate the meeting. The thing that impressed me was that he seemed ahead of the other managers. He not only did his homework and research, but he did it better and faster than the others. Of course, the others did not have Earl's ability to manage."

The assemblies also served another purpose. It was the method used to determine which athletes played at each level.

"Earl was a pretty good poker player," said McLaughlin. "He knew a good ball player when he saw one. Naturally, he was trying to get the best he could for his team, something the other managers did, too. But once again Earl was a little better than most at it. Looking back, I can see where he would play this game. He would have his eye on one guy, but he would talk up another player so the other managers would take him and leave Earl with the guy he wanted."

Fitzgerald, Georgia is a town of 8,015 in the south–central part of the state. It is near nothing, unless you consider Tifton a noteworthy landmark, and lies about two hours south of Macon and three hours west of Savannah. No matter, there is no reason for a baseball fan to stop there. The minor league team has gone the way of the stadium. Both have disappeared without a trace, and it is impossible to believe that either existed.

The Georgia–Florida League consisted of towns like Fitzgerald, Albany, Waycross, Tifton, and Valdosta, where you had no problems deciding where to eat. In Fitzgerald, the one restaurant was called the Spotted Pig and was located in an old railroad dining car.

This is where it all began for Weaver. Here he would be recognized as a major league managerial prospect even though his team had started well and faded to fourth place. This would be the first and last time he would have a losing record, finishing 65–74 as the team attracted 18,046 for the entire season, an average of 250 a game.

"Earl did pretty well that first season," said McLaughlin. "But he had a lot to learn. He always had a mathematical mind, but that's not to say he is a whiz in math. Rather, he understood the meaning of statistics and how to apply them. Early in his managing career he viewed baseball more as an art form. Later he discovered how to use data and make it work for him, and that is when he really came on. Of course, he matured over the years. He was just 26 when he started managing."

While veteran Weaver observers insist that he has mellowed, he still is a stick of dynamite around umpires. Earl's clashes with the game's arbiters are not just renowned in the majors, they are a part of minor league folklore. For example, one night in Waycross when he was calling the shots for Fitzgerald, he discovered that he was far more successful with his mouth than with his fists.

Like most Class D managers, Earl also played in the games.

Waycross is located on the edge of the Okefenokee Swamp, and the members of that team were especially obnoxious. Perhaps it was because they had to watch out for snakes, monstrous roaches, and vicious, blood-sucking mosquitoes. Those who toiled in Waycross say you had to be constantly on guard against creatures from the swamp, for it was not uncommon for snakes to crawl into the clubhouse during the night and curl up in a glove or batting helmet. If you weren't careful, you could end up with a copperhead on your head.

This story has several versions, depending upon the source. It seems that Weaver hit a pop-up, and as he ran down the first base line Waycross players in the dugout screamed, "Watermelon Head," a name which sent him into a rage. After the ball was caught, Earl dashed to the Waycross dugout and dove at his adversaries. They ducked and he landed on the bench, separating his right shoulder. "That was the last fight I ever got into," says Earl.

In 1958, Weaver returned to the Georgia–Florida League. Because Fitzgerald's populace stayed away from the games in droves, its franchise was shifted to Dublin, a town of 18,000 about 75 miles north, where Earl led Dublin to a third place finish and a 72–56 mark. The team attracted 31,704 fans that year and Weaver battled umpires over every decision that went against his team.

"Right from the start, Earl was in trouble with umpires," said Harry Dalton, who was the Orioles Assistant Minor League Director in the late 1950s. "W.T. Anderson was the president of the Georgia–Florida League then, and he would get reports about Earl kicking dirt on home plate or shaking his finger in the face of an umpire. Weaver was getting ejected about 6–8 times a year and fined $50 for each one. When he got in serious trouble with the umpires, I would go in and talk to him. Usually our meeting would end up with Earl trying to convince me that he was right and the umpires were wrong. He would say he was victimized, and usually he was."

"Earl is a perfectionist," said Jim McLaughlin. "He could understand a player's limitations. That always was one of his great strengths. He could understand that guys in Class D could not do things like major leaguers. But he never extended that tolerance to the umpires. He would not admit that they were as prone to mistakes as the Class D players. That is the interesting paradox about Earl. He expects umpires to be perfect, and in the minors there are some who are very bad because they are just starting, too. You see, Earl never had a Class D intellect. He was first rate and he thought the umpires in the Georgia–Florida League and everywhere elso should also be that way.

"We used to argue about this. He was impatient with the umpires and I was impatient with the way he acted toward them. I used to tell him to cut it out, that umpires make mistakes just like ballplayers. But he never saw it that way. It was not in his makeup."

Weaver says that it was in his season at Dublin when he grasped one of managing's great secrets.

"I learned that you can't ask a player to do something that is beyond his ability," he explained. "For example, when I had Boog Powell I couldn't expect him to steal bases. He had no speed. If you play a guy who is weak defensively because he hits home runs, you can't criticize him for making physical errors. It sounds simple, but it is a very important concept."

In 1959, Earl was promoted to Class C Aberdeen of the Northern League. There, his team went 69–55 and ended up in second place.

"After a couple years of managing, I could see that there was something special about Earl," said Harry Dalton. "He was improving each season. After a while it dawned on me that he would make a helluva major league manager."

Weaver made believers out of the Orioles' front office in 1960. His Fox Cities Class B Three-I League club won the title with an 82–56 record. The Three-I League was so named because all the teams were located in Indiana, Iowa, and Illinois, except Fox

Cities, which was in Appleton, Wisconsin. Fox Cities captured the pennant with two weeks left in the season.

"We had a tremendous team at Fox Cities," recalls Dean Chance, "including a number of guys who became Big Leaguers like myself, Pete Ward, Buster Narum, and Boog Powell. We were a powerhouse. We had talent. But some of the credit has to go to Earl. He never made a mistake. Personally, I think the guy is a genius."

Chance was drafted for $175,000 out of the Orioles' farm system by the Angels in the 1961 expansion draft. In 1964 he went on to win the Cy Young Award with a 20–9 record and a 1.65 earned run average. His 10-year career ended in 1970 with a 128–115 mark.

Today, Dean Chance travels the Midwest carnival circuit. He owns three booths. One has plates set up on a wooden ledge. Scowling faces are painted on them with the words, "Hit me," in the middle. If you break two plates with one softball, you win a two-foot Snoopy dog in a blue jump suit. Another of his attractions challenges you to throw a softball into a small-necked milk can. The prize is a stuffed St. Bernard.

After leaving baseball, Chance managed a fighter named Ray Anderson, whose smooth face and body were far more suited to modeling than boxing. Chance was later indicted in a fight-fixing scandal, but was found innocent.

Dean claims to be the world's greatest card player. During the middle 1970s he was reported to be operating a floating gin rummy game in the back of a 1959 Pontiac hearse in his native Wooster, Ohio. Chance denies this, although several of his friends relish telling the tale, and it was made public by *Cleveland Plain Dealer* sportswriter Dan Coughlin. Coughlin also says that Chance is one of the few men in Wooster ever to be rejected by the Elks Club. A card game in which Chance cleaned out several members led to the cold shoulder.

In many ways, Chance is Weaver's kind of guy. He is fun-loving and an excellent competitor, with an ego the size of the Goodyear blimp. But Earl was never as free with his money as Chance.

"I remember Earl Sidney Weaver very well," says Chance. "God, how he hated to be called Earl Sidney. We did it just to piss him off. In fact, his three favorite words were shit, fuck, and piss."

"Earl was never very subtle," adds Chance. "He was always on everybody's ass—his players, the opposition, and the umpires. When I joined the team, he already had a reputation as the kind of guy who didn't take much crap. You didn't step out of line when you played for Earl. Harry Dalton was his angel. Harry loved him. If it wasn't for Harry, I don't think Earl ever would have gotten a chance to manage in the majors.

"I was 19 when I played for Earl. I had just signed and I thought I was the greatest pitcher in the world. I wanted to pitch every fourth day. Earl had a five-man rotation, and that was it. We argued about it, but he said he had five starters, not four, and if I didn't like it, I could get the hell out. I respected him for that.

"His team meetings were something else. One day, he called us together and started using his three favorite words. We couldn't figure out what was wrong. Then he got real quiet. 'Okay,' he says. 'Which one of you sons of bitches propositioned the black elevator girl at the hotel?' All of us busted up laughing but one. Earl had his man.

"We had the worst team bus in the world. It was not air conditioned and was always breaking down. We would sit on the road for a couple hours at a time while the driver and Cal Ripken, our catcher, would be under the hood trying to fix it. I remember us calling the driver, 'No Doze,' because he was always taking those pills to stay awake while driving. The bus never went over 45 mph. It was amazing we got anywhere. After we won the pennant they gave us a new bus.

"But my favorite Earl story is this: One night we were playing in Burlington, and Earl knew I liked to play cards. He had me get into an all-night poker game with six Burlington players. He didn't care if I stayed up all night because I wasn't pitching the next day. But he wanted me to get Bob Priddy in the game because he was pitching for Burlington. The game went until 4 A.M. Priddy was so exhausted the next day that he fell asleep in the dugout. Yeah, we won that game. You have to love playing for a guy like Earl. He gives you 150%, is a great guy, and he never misses a trick."

Another member of that Fox Cities championship team was Pat Gillick. Now the General Manager of the Toronto Blue Jays, Gillick was Weaver's pitching ace. He won 10 straight games and had an 11–2 record.

"Earl was very energetic," recalls Gillick. "He would get to the park very early, and he did more than his share in terms of hitting fungos and throwing batting practice. But what struck me the most was that he came out of retirement to play a few games for us when we had a bunch of injuries. Earl had stopped playing full-time after that first year in Fitzgerald.

"Anyhow, we were running out of players and Earl was in the lineup for four straight days. Twice in that span he got hit with pitches in order to get on base. I mean, he did it on purpose. He was the kind of guy to stick out his arm and let the pitch hit it just so he could get to first base. Something like that makes an impression on you."

Gillick also confirms the theory that Earl felt he was superior to bus drivers.

"We were playing in Sioux City and the bus driver and Earl really got into it," said Gillick. "Earl was hot. I never did know what it was all about."

According to Gillick, Earl said to the driver,

"Listen, I'm tired of this. You're fired."

"What for?" asked the driver. "You can't fire me."

"Get outta here," said Weaver. "You're gone."

"Then he asked Cal Ripken to get behind the wheel," explained Gillick. "We left the driver in Sioux City and Ripken drove us about 500 miles home."

The relationship between Weaver and Ripken was always strong, but it may have been cemented that night. Ripken is now an Orioles coach and has been since 1975. He is the dean of the Baltimore coaching staff, others having retired or gone on to managing positions with different major league teams. Weaver marvels at Ripken's arm, which is strong and accurate. He may be the best batting practice pitcher in the majors in Weaver's opinion.

You can be sure of this much, as long as Earl is a manager Ripken will have a spot on his coaching staff. He is a friend, a hard worker, and a man Weaver trusts. It was a bond sealed in the tank towns of the Three-I League. Ripken was always there when Weaver called. Whether he had to catch a doubleheader or drive the bus, Ripken handled the chore.

"If you came through for Earl, he remembered it," says Gillick. "I'll tell you, everything Earl did was calculated. For example, the way he goes at it with the umpires or Jim Palmer is always done with something in mind. When he and Palmer get into a screaming match on the mound, the Orioles are usually up by five runs and Jim is missing the strike zone. Earl will say, 'You are the best pitcher in baseball, a goddamn Hall of Famer, now throw the ball over the plate.' Palmer will get mad and say something back and then Earl will say something. It makes Palmer more interested and he usually pitches better.

"I'll give you an example of Earl's shrewdness. I remember this night game. My girlfriend was in town. We went out for a while after the game and then decided to go to an all-night greasy spoon to get some breakfast. It was the only place open 24 hours. Well, we were eating and Earl walked in. We had a curfew and I was late. I expected Earl to come over and say something to me. I figured this is it, I'm done. He'll get me now. But he ignored me. Then the bill came. It was for $54.80. The food was $4.80 and Earl had tacked on $50 for breaking curfew. You know, he was something else.

"Another thing about Earl was that they called him 'Doodles' when he played in New Orleans. He hated it. It was after the comic strip character, Doodles Weaver. If you wanted to get him mad, you could just call him Doodles."

After winning his league pennant in 1960, Weaver was put in charge of formulating the spring practice drills and routines for the Orioles' minor league system from Class AA down. Admirers of Earl often mention his "Oriole Book." It is the Baltimore way of doing things, strong on defense and pitching. Mental mistakes are greeted like the Bill of Rights in the Kremlin. In truth, there is no Oriole Book in that form. But there is a training program devised by Weaver in the spring of 1961 and adopted throughout the entire system a few years later. It is still being used today.

Earl's Fox Cities team fell to fourth place with a 67–62 mark in 1961. His biggest victory of the year came when he won a protest over a restraining line. That is the last time a protest has gone in Weaver's favor. During that season, Earl said he came close to quitting. He had a run-in with the umpires and was fined $50 by Three-I League President Vern Hoscheit. Hoscheit banned him from managing until his debt was paid.

"I managed the next night," recalled Weaver. "Harry Dalton

came to see me and calmed me down. I think I sent a check to pay the fine, but they never cashed it."

In 1962 Weaver was promoted to Class A Elmira, New York, where he spent the next four summers. In that upstate New York town he would find a new wife, a new winter profession, a new home, and pull a new stunt that would carry far beyond the Eastern League.

"They still love me in Elmira," says Weaver. "In Rochester they get down on me when the Orioles call up some of their players to the big leagues. They blame it on me. But in Elmira, it's a different story."

That first year in Elmira was nothing special. The team finished in second place, but its record was only 72–68. Earl was Earl, fighting with umpires, screaming at his players and making the most out of what had been given to him. Never was that truer than in the case of Steve Dalkowski. Dalkowski was a legend. His name still rolls off the tongues of older scouts and managers.

"Yeah, the kid you're talking about can throw hard," a scout would say. "But remember Steve Dalkowski. No one threw harder than Dalkowski." Yes, they say, no one. Not Bob Feller, not Nolan Ryan, not Sandy Koufax, not Walter Johnson, not J.R. Richard.

Dalkowski signed his first pro contract in 1957. He was 18. He was released in 1966, a washout at 27 with a 46–80 record and a 5.67 ERA to show for nine aimless years in the minors. The man said to have the strongest arm in the history of the game went 1–8 with an 8.13 ERA at Kingsport, 3–12 with an 8.39 ERA at Tri-Cities, and 7–15 with a 5.14 ERA at Pensacola. He never made it to the majors and was 2–3 with a 7.12 ERA in Class AAA.

Dalkowski stories are legion. One night in Pensacola, he threw three straight pitches over the heads of the batter, catcher, and umpire. Another time one of his heaves went through a fence 30 feet behind home plate.

Now we are approaching the heart of Dalkowski's problem. In 995 professional innings he fanned 1,396 batters. He also walked 1,354. If a pitcher strikes out one hitter per inning, he has outstanding speed. Dalkowski wasn't just fast, he was dangerous. That was especially true when you consider his lack of control. Any time he delivered a pitch it could have killed or maimed a batter. He had no idea where it was going and it moved at speeds that were lethal.

Imagine the high school kids who faced Dalkowski in the minors. In one game he pitched a no-hitter and struck out 18. He also walked 18. There are tales of a batter's ear allegedly knocked off by Dalkowski's fastball, and an umpire who was hit by a pitch and quit the profession. There are stories of broken bats, backstops, screens, and who knows what else—all supposedly destroyed by Dalkowski's fastball.

No one can separate lore from fact. Let it suffice that he was the greatest unharnessed pitching talent ever to set foot on the diamond. Consider some of his numbers: in 62 innings at Kingsport he fanned 121, walked 129, and threw 39 wild pitches. He holds the Northern League record for the most strikeouts and walks in a game—21.

Dalkowski received $4,000 to sign with the Orioles. He had terrible eyesight and wore glasses thicker than the bottoms of soda bottles. He was shy, almost introverted. His fastball once smashed the skull of a player in the Appalachian League and the batter never played again. It is said that Dalkowski often worried that he might deliver another such pitch and was terrified that it would kill someone. The Orioles tried everything to improve his accuracy. They had him throw at a wooden target. They had him throw for 45 minutes straight until he was exhausted, believing his aim would improve as his velocity diminished. They had him throw to the plate with batters standing in both the left and right batters' boxes.

They clocked the speed of his delivery and he came in at 93 mph. Bob Feller scored at 98.6 mph. Some say this proves Dalkowski's speed was nothing but hype. They forget to mention that it took Dalkowski 10 minutes to throw a pitch straight enough to be measured. Furthermore, he had to slow it down to get it near the timing device. Those present agree that many of Dalkowski's errant tosses were well over 100 mph.

Steve Dalkowski would be Earl Weaver's project at Elmira. As with many pitchers, Dalkowski would never perform better than under Weaver.

"When Steve joined the team, there was nothing I could tell him," said Weaver. "Hell, he had gotten every piece of advice, tried everything, and had the best pitching coaches in the world talk to him. What was I going to say? So I didn't say anything. I just let him pitch."

Suddenly, Dalkowski's offerings were around home plate. For the first time in his career, he walked fewer batters than innings pitched. He finished with a 7–10 record and a 3.04 ERA. He had six shutouts and eight complete games. In 160 innings, he walked 114 and fanned 190. Later, he would give Weaver credit for his success.

But success was short-lived. Dalkowski injured his arm the next season, and his career was not helped by his nocturnal activities. Four times Weaver had to bail him out of jail. On several other occasions he discovered Dalkowski passed out on the front lawn of his boarding house. Steve seldom rebelled against the flood of advice he was given, as if drinking was his protest sign. After leaving baseball he continued to experience hard times. He bummed around California, working as a migrant fruit picker. Occasionally, he calls Weaver, usually after he has spent some time in a tavern. *Baltimore Sun* baseball writer Ken Nigro scored a journalistic coup when he tracked down Dalkowski in 1979. Dalkowski openly discussed his bouts with drinking, his failed marriage and, lastly, his appreciation for Weaver. When Dalkowski's name is mentioned all Earl can do is shake his head and say, "He was the fastest pitcher I ever saw."

During his five years at Elmira Weaver would manage many of the players who composed the great Baltimore teams of the late 1960s and early 1970s. Eddie Watt, Dave McNally, Dave Leonhard, Andy Etchebarren, Mark Belanger, and Paul Blair all played under Weaver on the Class A Eastern League team. But the most important event of his stay in Elmira would happen off the field.

"I wasn't making much money back then, $5–6,000 a year," he said. "I would take $75 and try to make it last 15 days. By the middle of May in 1963, I was down to $10 and I called my wife to see if I could write a check. She told me that she was getting a divorce. Our entire savings and checking accounts were gone. I was 33 and had $10 to my name when I started over."

A year later, Earl married his current wife, Marianna, a secretary in Elmira. During most of their courtship, Marianna knew

Earl more as a used car salesman than as the manager of the Elmira Pioneers.

"Don't kid yourself, I was a damn good salesman," said Weaver. "I knew all the tricks when it came to selling cars. I knew when to leave the customers alone so they could talk among themselves and I knew when to press hard for a sale."

If all of this sounds boastful, it should be mentioned that the records also back Earl up. Let's face it, the man knows better than to say something if the numbers tell another story. "It ain't braggin' if you done it," to quote one of Weaver's old favorites from the Gas House Gang, Dizzy Dean.

So it was with Earl. He and Marianna purchased a home in Elmira largely because of Earl's knack in auto sales. Weaver also became addicted to gardening in Elmira. The Pioneers' groundskeeper was Pat Santarone, a man who loves the soil. Soon Weaver and Santarone were discussing the joy of dirt running through their fingers and watching something grow from a seed. Santarone transformed Weaver into a gardener. The two men engaged in tomato-growing contests and Earl turned much of his backyard into a garden. It became his major hobby, and it blossomed further when Weaver and Santarone were both promoted to the Orioles.

"At that time, I thought I would spend the rest of my life in Elmira," said Weaver. "I never had any serious thought of managing in the majors. I was an organization man, a guy to take care of things down on the farm."

But the Orioles had other ideas. They were impressed by Earl's four-year record in Elmira. Under him the Pioneers had won one pennant and were second three times.

Meanwhile, Earl continued to make life miserable for the umpires. In one game an umpire blew a call at third base. At least, that is what Weaver claimed. The usual argument ensued, with Weaver acting as though fate had again blinded the umpires and denied his team its just reward. Finally Earl had enough. He picked up third base and carried it into the dugout, then into the clubhouse, locking the door.

"He was in there for 10 minutes with it," said Harry Dalton. "They had to send a member of the ground crew to get it. This was not the last time he would pull something like that."

As Weaver and the umpires continued their war, Dalton sent

George Bamberger to "cool down Earl." Bamberger was an old friend of Earl's and he also served as the Orioles' Minor League Pitching Coach.

"Bamberger spent a week with Earl and told me that Earl had fallen in love," said Dalton. "Bamberger reported that Earl was a changed man. He had really mellowed. He was absolutely great with the umpires."

The following week Dalton traveled to Elmira.

"As soon as I walked into the park I saw a sight I'll never forget," said Dalton. "There was Earl sitting on top of home plate, his arms folded. All the umpires were standing around him, shaking their fingers in his face. Earl just sat there like a sphinx. I called Bamberger the next day and told him that he might be a great pitching coach, but he was a lousy judge of managers. Then I told him what I had seen and we both laughed."

The Orioles also had Earl run Baltimore's entry in the winter Instructional League. Each team plays about 40 games and is composed of precocious prospects from the farm system. The season begins in late October and is over by December. Little attention is paid to game scores, the emphasis being on individual development and teaching. Earl was strong in those areas or he never would have been named to this crucial post, and he carried his job one step further. He wanted to win.

"One day we were playing Earl's team in Clearwater," recalls former Cubs Manager Charley Grimm. "Earl was bitching at the umpires, holding up the game and all that. Finally I yelled at him, 'Hey, Weaver! You want first place? You can have it. We'll take second. This is the instructional league. What the hell is wrong with you?' " Earl ignored Grimm's remarks and continued his tirade.

While working during the winter increased Earl's stock with the Orioles, he feels it hurt his personal life.

"I was away from home 10 months out of the year," said Weaver. "I think that is a big reason my first marriage broke up."

In 1966, the Birds thought Weaver was ready for something more. He had not suffered a losing season since Fitzgerald, in 1957, and he had never finished lower that fourth. That persuaded the Orioles to place him in charge of their Class AAA Rochester club.

"Earl was a very good minor league manager," said Harry Dalton. "He could size up a player as well as anyone I have ever seen. He could break down a player's strengths and weaknesses well, something you look for in a minor league manager. He also was a good teacher. He turned in outstanding reports."

"When I was in Rochester, Earl Weaver was just what we needed," said Carl Steinfeldt, now the general manager of the Charleston [South Carolina] Charlies. "I was the assistant general manager in 1966 when Earl came to us. We had not won a pennant in 13 years. The team was near bankruptcy. We lost $100,000 in 1965. In 1966, there was no way we should have won the championship. The talent was not there, but Earl got us into first place. We went from $100,000 in the hole to $40,000 in the black, and a lot of that credit has to go to Earl Weaver."

In 1966, Rochester drew 273,247 fans. Weaver was their favorite.

"The team was owned by Manny Silver, and he wanted to hold a day for Earl in 1967," recalled Steinfeldt. "Silver gave Earl a car and $5,000. Later, he called one of the players in and asked him what they were going to give Earl. They tried to take up a collection, but no one would give a thing. Silver went out and bought a color TV and told Earl it was from the players.

"I'll tell you why the players didn't like Earl. It was because he would kick them in the ass. They didn't like it, but most of them will admit now that Earl was right. He knew the players didn't love him, but he didn't give a damn. He'd yell and scream and do whatever it took to make them play better. He was trying to win a pennant, not a popularity contest."

Steinfeldt illustrates this point with a story about a pitcher named Jerry Herron.

"Herron was wild, walking guys all the time. I think it was the fourth inning of this one game, Herron was wild as usual. Earl was screaming at him. You could hear him yell, 'If you walk the next guy just pack your bags and go back to Elmira. I'm not even going to come out to the mound. Walk the next batter and you're gone. Just get the hell out and go to Elmira.'

"Sure enough, Herron walks the next batter. He looks to the dugout and Earl does not move. Then, Herron walks into the dugout and on into the clubhouse. The next day he left for Elmira.

"Weaver was the smartest and the most colorful manager in the minors. He was great for business. He would do anything the front office wanted. He made public appearances, met with the fans, and never forgot his roots. After he got to the majors, he would come back to Rochester and help if we needed a winter public appearance by him.

"Of course, Earl's record and what he did to the umpires are what made him great. He was very big on kicking dirt on home plate or one of the bases. He carried third base off the field, just like he did in Elmira. It was not unusual for helmets, bats, and towels to end up on the diamond when Earl was going at it in the dugout."

Several of his outbursts occurred in Richmond. On one occasion, he buried home plate under a hill of dust. In another game he protested the music blaring while the game was taking place, objecting that the organ did not stop even when the pitcher was throwing to the batters. The umpires ignored Earl and the fans booed him. The next time Rochester played in Richmond it was billed as "Earl Weaver Annoyance Day." The fans carried every imaginable musical instrument and banged, blew, and played away whenever a Rochester batter came to bat.

There was a game in Rochester when Earl thought the umpire had missed a call on a checked swing.

"We don't even get a strike when the batter swings," Weaver screamed at the umpire.

The umpire said nothing.

"They must have changed the rules," roared Weaver. "I bet you guys got your own rulebook. I'd like to read that book one day."

"Can you read?" the umpire shouted at Weaver.

At the same moment, the batter hit a pitch and was running to first base, as was the umpire.

"I can't read your book," Weaver said to the umpire. "Because it is in Braille."

Even though the play was still in progress, the umpire stopped.

"Get outta here, Weaver," said the umpire.

Earl walked onto the field. He told the umpire that he was just "getting off a good line. You made a joke and so did I." The man in blue did not have a sense of humor to match Weaver's, and Earl was thumbed again.

The heist of third base followed a call by an umpire on a fair ball. Weaver again thought the umpire had erred. Words, then shouts, then screams were exchanged. Earl was ejected. He picked up the base and carried it off with him, telling the umpire that he might as well take it since it obviously meant nothing to the umpires.

Perhaps the most bizarre Weaver–umpire incident was revealed by Earl to the *Baltimore Evening Sun* in 1971. It took place in 1966, when Weaver's Rochester club was playing Columbus.

"Home plate umpire Augie Guglielmi was making some terrible calls," recalls Weaver. "We were losing by a run and I was about to blow my top. I went out to talk to him, then I decided to get him to blow his instead. I said, 'Oh little man, the game has passed you by.' That did it. He started swearing and threw me out, but since he was the one acting up, I said to him, 'I ain't leaving. You can call a cop if you want or you can forfeit the game.'

"Wilbur Wood was the pitcher and we used to hit him pretty good. Still, I wasn't going to leave. The other umpires, I think Ron Luciano was one of them, came running in from first and third as I stood on the plate. Just as they got there Guglielmi yelled out to Wood to throw the ball."

"You should have seen them scatter. Steve Demeter was our hitter and as soon as he heard the ump's instruction he hurried into the batter's box. I jumped straight into the air and headed to the dugout."

"When the umpire told me to throw the ball I figured I would, since it would be called a strike if it was anywhere near the plate," said Wood. "I wound up and just as I was ready to throw Weaver ran across the plate and I hitched my delivery. I threw it and Demeter hit the ball into right field."

"Demeter got a double or a triple," says Weaver. "He knocked in two runs with it and we went ahead to win the game. Remember, I had been thrown out, so I'm leaving. Then, [Columbus Manager] Larry Shepard comes steaming out of the dugout, asking Guglielmi what he was going to do now. What could he do? He said pitch, the ball was hit, and a couple of runs scored. I know one thing, not too many guys on defense were ready."

During this period of his career Weaver was engaged in a number of intense pennant races. In 1963 and 1965, his team won the championship on the last day of the season. They lost it on the final day of 1964 and 1966. In 1967, they tied for the title.

"We got beat in a playoff game in 1967," said Carl Steinfeldt. "We were playing Richmond and a guy named Jim Britton was pitching against us. He was going great. In the seventh inning he received a standing ovation from the crowd. His father was in the stands and while cheering suffered a heart attack and died. Britton beat us and did not find out what had happened to his dad until after the game."

Weaver's wins in Rochester drew the attention of those who ran the winter baseball leagues in Latin America and he was named manager of the Santurce club in Puerto Rico. That meant an extra $6,000 to Weaver, but it also got him into a contract dispute with Harry Dalton.

"Harry wanted to cut my salary from $8,600 to $7,000 because I was going to winter ball instead of managing the Instructional League team," said Earl. "Dalton said he was getting two months less work out of me. I agreed on that point, but I pointed out I had been around a long time." When it was over, Earl settled for $8,000.

"The first time I ever saw Earl was in winter ball after the 1966 season," says Elrod Hendricks, now an Orioles coach. "We didn't hit it off on the first day. I was taking batting practice and was used to swinging for 20 minutes. Earl let me have ten swings and then he stood right in front of me, asking me if I was going to take 50 swings or what. I told him that I just might, so he ordered the pitcher to stop throwing to me.

"I got pissed and went to the outfield and would not come in when he called me to take batting practice later in the day. That left us in a standoff. He didn't play me for a month. He was using pitchers like Ruben Gomez and Juan Pizzaro to pinch hit instead of me. Then one day he sent me up to bat and I hit a homer to win the game. I sat for another week before getting another chance. Again I homered. After that I was in the lineup regularly."

In light of this incident it is surprising to learn that Elrod Hendricks probably was Earl's favorite player. He brought Elrod up to the majors and has kept him in the Orioles organization ever since, making sure to reacquire him whenever he was traded. This illustrates the maturity and willingness to change that

Weaver has demonstrated over the years and helped to convince Harry Dalton that Weaver was ready to be brought to Baltimore in 1968.

4

The Manager

Earl Weaver sat in the corner of the dugout. His small body was lost in the Orioles' billowy vinyl jacket.

The Birds were taking batting practice. It was two hours before the game and Weaver stared intently at the field, puffing on a Raleigh. Now was the time for him to play the philosopher—king, the one man in baseball who knows it all. Spending an hour with Weaver in the dugout before a game is like taking a course in Managing 101. Earl believes that his job not only consists of answering reporters' questions but of putting the game in context, explaining its nuances and spreading the baseball gospel according to Weaver. Listening to him is a treat. Baltimore reporters who have followed him for a decade say he continually comes up with something new.

"I think I like baseball best when I listen to Earl before a game," said Merrell Whittlesey, a former *Washington Star* baseball writer for more than 20 years. "Earl's insights are amazing, and he has a great sense of humor."

Earl rules the dugout. It is here that he educates the press, his players, and his coaches. He is not one for meetings. When something needs to be done or said, it takes place in the dugout. Like on the team bus, no one sits next to Earl.

Some come near, but not too close. You can tell that Weaver prefers it that way.

On this day a young reporter asks Weaver what makes the Orioles farm system unique. It not only has produced the players who have given Baltimore the best record in baseball over the last 24 years, it turns out managers. Earl was the first to come through the organization and rise to the top like a prized prospect. But there are many others who have spent time in the minors for the Birds and/or coached under Weaver.

Joe Altobelli and Ken Boyer followed Weaver as manager of the Rochester Red Wings. Altobelli was the Giants' skipper for a time and Boyer ran the Cardinals for two years. Billy Hunter, Jim Frey, George Bamberger, and Frank Robinson served as Earl's coaches in addition to putting in time down on the farm. Frey managed the Royals, Robinson has the Giants, Hunter managed Texas for a time, and only a heart condition forced Bamberger to retire as Milwaukee's manager. (Bamberger has since recovered and is currently manager of the New York Mets.)

"We have had a lot of good men," said Weaver. "But the key is that we have kept things together in the organization. Whenever a coach leaves, we replace him with someone from our farm system. That serves two purposes. It tells the guys down there that they can move up if they do a good job, and it keeps the continuity intact. We have a certain way of doing things and everyone does things the same. It keeps everything simple and running smoothly."

Ah yes, the old KISS (Keep It Simple, Stupid) theory. It is one of Weaver's canons. He may have an impressive intellect, but he knows that few ballplayers are Phi Beta Kappas. Besides, you don't have to be smart to play the game intelligently. Babe Ruth proved that. And intelligence is no guarantee of stardom. College players like Steve Hovely (called "egghead" by his teammates) illustrate this point. Add to this another Weaverism: "You can be smart and be a dumb player or be dumb and be a smart player, but the player or manager who does best is one with good baseball judgment."

Baseball judgment.

It is a phrase Earl beats to death. It encompasses picking your team and your coaches. It includes knowing how to use your statistics and your bench, how to keep the umpires sharp without alienating them, and how to deal with the press. Most of all, it means looking at a player and knowing what he can and cannot do and how you can best use him.

Listening to Weaver helps, but baseball judgment is something that must be practiced. So you go to Bluefield, West Virginia, where the Orioles gather 35 raw rookies each summer. Or you spend a few summers in Charlotte or Rochester. Along the way, your skin turns to leather and wrinkles form around your eyes from squinting at the players in the sun. You pay your dues, as Weaver did. And if everyone is paying the same dues under the same system, that elusive quality, baseball judgment, is honed.

"Here is how it worked," said Weaver. "George Bamberger was the Orioles' Minor League Pitching Coach when I managed in the minors. We both came to Baltimore in 1968 as coaches. When I took over as manager, George and I set up a program for the pitchers. It was also put into our farm system. When George left to manage the Brewers, we brought up Ray Miller. He was our Minor League Pitching Coach. He had been in George's footsteps in the minors, carrying out the same program. It is the same up and down the organization. One of the important things is that everybody does it the same way. If not, you end up with confusion and injuries."

Of course, Weaver's presence at the top of this ladder is the reason so many of his coaches have left the Orioles. There was no room to make that last step. Also, there is a certain mystique surrounding a coach under Weaver. Many baseball executives say that a few years on the Orioles farms and then working with Weaver comprise the ideal manager-trainee program. That is why so many have been hired and why Ray Miller is said to be the next Orioles coach who will become a manager.

In the late 1960s and the 1970s, the Orioles' minor league organization was more fertile than the best Iowa farmland. Through the ranks came Boog Powell, Dave Johnson, Mark Belanger, Dave McNally, Bobby Grich, Don Baylor, Eddie Watt, Jim Palmer, Wayne Garland, Andy Etchebarren, Doug DeCinces, Eddie Murray, Mike Flanagan, Paul Blair, Al Bumbry, Rich Coggins, Terry Crowley, Merv Rettenmund, Rich Dauer, Tom Phoebus, and many more. Weaver deserves a certain amount of credit for the bumper crop, but most should go to Jim McLaughlin, Harry Dalton, Jim Russo, and the battery of Baltimore scouts.

Yes, Weaver is a great manager, and it helps that he came to Baltimore at the right time. Dalton moved into the general manager's position in 1966. From the day he left the minor league department and walked into the GM's office, many insist his top priority was to make Weaver manager of the Orioles. As Dean Chance has said, "Dalton was Earl's angel."

At that time the Orioles had a competent manager in Hank Bauer. He assumed those duties in 1964 and watched the Birds average 95 wins for two years, good for third place each time. Bauer was an old marine with a chiseled, often frightening face and a crew cut. He had played for the Yankees in the 1950s and been a fine hitting outfielder. Previously, he had managed the Kansas City Athletics. You could do far worse than Hank Bauer for a manager.

Dalton knew this. That was why he brought Bauer back for 1966. He also promoted Weaver from Elmira to Class AAA Rochester for the 1966 season. That way, Earl's next logical step upward would be Baltimore. But Bauer surprised everyone by leading the Birds to their first-ever American League pennant and World Series triumph in 1966. It came a dozen years after the franchise crawled out of St. Louis, leaving the nickname "Browns" behind.

The 1966 Orioles were a magnificent team. They swept the heavily favored Dodgers in four straight games to become World Champions. They had a pitching staff of young lions with Wally Bunker, Palmer, McNally, and Phoebus. Frank Robinson was obtained during the winter for Milt Pappas and went on to become the MVP. Brooks Robinson was an astounding third baseman. The infield and outfield were solid. Basically, it was a young team with a touch of age. That is the perfect combination, one which gives a team wisdom and zest.

But in 1967 something went wrong. The Birds finished a distant sixth, with a dismal 76–85 record. Of course, there were excuses. A big one was Palmer's arm ailment which caused him to slip all the way back to Class A.

"There was more to it than injuries." said Jim Russo. "Late in 1967, Harry Dalton had me follow the team for two weeks. Usually I was out ahead of the club, watching the teams we would play next and then filing reports on them. This time I focused on the Orioles. First of all, you could see they were not in good physical condition. After winning the Series, they had become complacent. Even Brooks Robinson, as great and as dedicated a player as he was, had gotten overweight. The problem was obvious, but the coaches and manager were too close to see it. This was the first time we thought of making Earl the manager."

Some say that Dalton wanted to replace Bauer with Weaver before 1968. It would have been a controversial decision since Bauer had had three fine years in Baltimore before the slide of 1967. Instead, Dalton decided to change the coaching staff. Weaver and George Bamberger were promoted from the minors and Sherman Lollar, Harry Brecheen, and Gene Woodling were fired. This did not sit well with Bauer, who was personally fond of the three men. A manager usually chooses his own coaches with a minimum of front office interference. This was the first sign that Bauer was in serious trouble.

As soon as he was made a coach, I think we all knew that Earl would be the manager eventually" said Brooks Robinson. "He was Harry Dalton's boy. He had put together a great record in the minors. It was obvious that he was more than a first-base coach."

"Bauer didn't like it when Earl joined his staff," said Russo. "He thought Earl was brought in as heir apparent, but that was not the case. Earl had been successful with many of the Orioles in the minors. We felt he could help them at the major league level. We thought he would be effective with Boog Powell, who needed a push and some of Earl's psychology."

"When I became the Orioles General Manager, in the back of

my mind I had the idea I would like to make Weaver the manager," admitted Harry Dalton. "But we won the pennant in 1966 with Hank Bauer, and it was a great thing for the city of Baltimore. When we had a miserable season in 1967, I decided to make a change on the coaching staff. Weaver and George Bamberger had had a promotion coming their way for some time. When we got off to a slow start in 1968, I began seriously thinking of turning the team over to Earl. By early June, I was convinced that Bauer was not doing the job. Even though he was an ex-marine and had this tough guy reputation, he was a very sweet person underneath and he was letting the club drift away from him."

Meanwhile, Earl insisted that being the Orioles first-base coach "was the best job I ever had. I was in the majors, getting in time toward my pension. It was nice."

Bauer and Earl were not exactly drinking pals. The two men kept their distance, Earl taking care to hit fungos, throw batting practice, and handle the other mundane chores that ready a team for a game. They did their jobs and kept out of each other's way.

On one occasion Bauer did ask Weaver to talk hitting with Boog Powell. "He was worried about Boog's frame of mind," said Earl. "I didn't do that much. We discussed his hitting and I made a few suggestions about his stance. Boog really wasn't interested. That was about the extent of it."

Earning $15,000 and relishing the major league expense account money and first class travel and lodging after 20 years of beating the bushes, Earl admitted to being "happier than a pig in slop. I'd watch Bauer getting nervous when our pitchers got hit or when we didn't hit, and I was happy that I didn't have to deal with all those pressures. I still did not think I would manage in the majors," he claims.

Although Weaver still maintains that he harbored no big league managerial ambitions, it rings hollow. He was always a man of drive and superior intelligence, and it is hard to imagine him being content with the simple life of a first-base coach for very long.

"In Earl's mind there was never a doubt he would be a major league manager, from the time he started in Fitzgerald," said Jim McLaughlin. "Just like there was never a doubt he'd make the majors as a player when he signed his first pro contract. He always aimed to be the best. That is a part of his makeup."

In early June of 1968, the Birds went 2–8 on a West Coast trip. Dalton and his staff met and evaluated the team. As a result they decided to give Bauer a little more time—but not much.

The Orioles continued to flounder, although they did win 7 of 10 and 9 of 14 before the All-Star break to raise their record to 43–37. It was too late for Bauer, however.

"I was at the All-Star game in Houston when I decided to go to Earl," recalled Dalton. "After the game, I stopped by Bauer's home in Kansas City. I told him I wanted to make the change. He was shocked and disappointed, and it hurt me because I liked Hank personally. From the Kansas City airport I called Earl and I told him I wanted to meet with him that night."

Weaver was at his apartment swimming pool when he was informed that Harry Dalton was on the telephone. Dalton would say only that he wanted to stop by to see Earl around 10 P.M. Weaver said nothing, but he knew what was in store. A general manager does not go to the home of a first-base coach to make sure the coach's arm is strong enough to throw batting practice the next day.

Word of Bauer's dismissal already was out. Most thought the position would go to Weaver, but some felt veteran third-base coach Billy Hunter might receive the nod.

"All I can say is that it isn't me," Hunter said when the *Baltimore Morning Sun* asked him about taking Bauer's place. "I don't know. Maybe I am supposed to be the Frank Crosetti of the Baltimore Orioles."

Hunter had been an Orioles coach since 1964, in addition to playing shortstop for the original Baltimore Orioles of 1954. He wanted to manage the Birds and was extremely disappointed to be passed over. His reference was to long-time Yankee coach Frank Crosetti, who was always available for managerial duties in New York but never was asked.

When Dalton arrived at Weaver's home he was wearing a huge smile.

"I've just gotten in from Kansas City," Dalton told Earl. "I want you to take over the club."

Earl asked immediately what salary the position would yield.

"I was stunned," says Dalton. "I expected Earl to stick out his hand and say something like 'That's great, let's go to work.' Instead, he asked how much I would pay him. I was surprised and taken aback. I knew Earl was a good negotiator, but I never expected anything like that."

They spent two hours talking dollars. The haggling was intense. Dalton's first offer was in the $20,000 range. Earl greeted it like the plague. In addition to his $15,000 coach's salary, at the time he could earn $7–10,000 for managing in winter ball, depending upon his team's success. "If I manage the Orioles, I can't go to winter ball," Weaver told Dalton. "That will cost me money. Ain't no way I'm going to manage your team for less money than I could make as a coach."

The dickering continued. The two men had been through this before. Dalton had wanted to cut Earl's income by $1,600 when he first started managing in Latin America during the winter. When that session was concluded, Weaver had talked his way into only a $600 pay cut, a major achievement according to those close to the situation.

Harry Dalton is a shrewd businessman and he wanted to keep his payroll low. Like all baseball men of the late 1960s he was fond of inexpensive help, but he had a tough foe in Earl. It is not easy to deal with a former used car salesman and loan officer. As Earl often says, "I've heard all the lines and stories."

"After a while I actually began to think Earl might not take the job," recalled Dalton. "It was impossible to comprehend Earl passing it up, but he argued that well. Eventually we came to a compromise, and we set up a press conference to announce the change the next day. We had Earl check into a hotel so the media wouldn't bother him before he had a chance to make an announcement." The final salary figure was $28,000. Earl is still proud of the way he conducted these negotiations.

Few were surprised on July 11, 1968 when Dalton named Weaver to manage the Orioles. All three Baltimore newspapers agreed that the change was needed, although Hank Bauer was an acceptable skipper. Everyone knew Bauer was not a Dalton favorite and the Birds had not performed well for the last 1½ seasons. They were 10½ games behind the Tigers when Bauer was relieved.

"I wanted a manager who would make things happen and keep a tighter rein over the players," said Dalton. "I knew Earl would not be afraid to make moves. He is an aggressive guy who doesn't back down for anyone."

"This is a brutal spot for Weaver," wrote the *Baltimore Evening Sun's* Phil Jackman. "He could be an absolute genius between now and October and the Tigers are still about 80% certain of being in the World Series . . . It has been a rough five months for Weaver, everybody knowing he was around to pick up the pieces once Bauer was let go. So now another guy joins the sleepless nights brigade and Bauer gets a paid vacation. It's a good life, but short."

Bauer's annual salary was $50,000. He had been American League Manager of the Year in 1964 and 1966. His contract was guaranteed through the 1968 season. Immediately after his axing, Bauer was diplomatic. "These things happen," he said. "I don't know why but they do. Let me say I more or less expected it. I didn't realize it would happen so soon. But I expected something after they fired my coaches last year. I have no ill-feeling towards the Baltimore Orioles. They treated me well and I was well paid."

Later, Bauer would change his gracious tone in an interview with Gordon Beard of the *Associated Press*. "I didn't want him [Weaver] around," Bauer told Beard. "I was knifed in the back once before." (The reference was to 1962 when Bauer was managing in Kansas City. The Athletics' owner, Charlie Finley, had hired Eddie Lopat to serve as pitching coach, but it was clear that Lopat was fated to succeed Bauer, and Bauer resigned before Finley could fire him.) "I see that Weaver was hired just for the rest of 1968," added Bauer. "They must not have much faith in him, either. I would have made Billy Hunter the manager. He knows the players better."

Bauer also indicated that Dalton had asked him to resign at the end of 1967. "I wasn't going to quit with a $50,000 contract, and that's why they didn't fire me [over the winter]. They didn't want to pay me off."

Again Bauer brought up the firing of his coaches. "Why not get rid of me instead of using the coaches as scapegoats? I was the guy running the show. Having Weaver around meant we had to get off to a fast start or I wouldn't be around long."

Dalton denies that he ever asked Bauer to quit, also explaining that Weaver was the first Orioles manager in the 14-year history of the franchise to climb throught the ranks of the farm system. In 1968 that was the exception. Now it is the rule for Orioles coaches.

Harry Dalton wanted a manager who would shake things up, and Weaver fit the bill. Earl's first announcement was to name Don Buford as starting centerfielder.

Buford was the only Oriole Earl could stare straight in the eye. At 5-foot-7 and 160 pounds, he would be considered small for a major league ballplayer. The Birds had obtained Buford from the White Sox prior to the 1968 season. In his last two years with Chicago he batted an uninspiring .244 and .241, with a total of 12 homers. Based on those numbers it is easy to understand Hank Bauer's reasons for using Buford as a spare part. The little guy was fast, but he was not a good outfielder and he didn't hit. In this case, one out of three wasn't enough to endear Buford to Bauer.

But there was something appealing about Buford. He had an engaging personality and he loved to play. He ran everywhere all the time. Baseball was his passion and he approached it with the zeal of Ponce de Leon in his quest for the Fountain of Youth. Weaver and Buford had more in common than stature.

In his maiden contest as the Orioles skipper, Weaver made Buford his leadoff batter and benched Paul Blair. A brilliant centerfielder who some say was the greatest gloveman ever to play the position, Blair was batting a miserable .196. "Given the choice, I will usually play an offensive player over a defensive one" Weaver often says.

He carried out this axiom with Buford and Blair, and it paid off immediately as the Orioles defeated Washington 2–0 in Earl's managerial debut. The Birds scored in the first inning when Senator starter Joe Coleman walked Buford. Buford moved to third on a Mark Belanger base hit and scored on a ground out. Buford then crushed a 400-foot homer off Coleman in the fifth for the other Baltimore run.

A romantic would say this demonstrates that Earl was a genius from the beginning. More logically, it displayed his penchant for putting the right man in the right spot and keeping the odds in favor of his team. Earl knew Coleman was the kind of pitcher Buford could handle, so he placed him in the lineup.

As the 1968 season continued, Buford proved he could hit

pitchers other than Joe Coleman. He finished the season with a
.282 batting average and 15 homers, three more than in the two
previous seasons combined. He also stole 27 bases and was the
main reason the Birds were an impressive 48–34 under Weaver.

Many insist Buford was Weaver's favorite Oriole, and there
were indeed several times when Earl went to great lengths to
protect him. The first was in a game with the White Sox in which
Buford was hit in the back with a pitch by Bart Johnson. Buford
physically challenged the 6-foot-6 Johnson because he was sure
Johnson had purposely thrown at him. After the game Weaver
so vigorously backed Buford that it led Johnson to threaten a
lawsuit.

"Johnson deliberately tried to maim one of my ballplayers and
he doesn't belong in the major leagues," Weaver was quoted in
the *Chicago Sun-Times*. "The man took the ball and deliberately
threw it at another human being with the intent to injure or
maim."

"If Earl Weaver ever says anything like that about me again, I'll
sue him for defamation of character," Johnson told *Chicago
Today*.

Weaver responded that he had been misquoted, citing a mixup
in semantics. Thus Weaver deftly covers his tracks by qualifying
inflamatory remarks with "if," or "suppose a pitcher . . . " Like
juggling his lineup or keeping umpires on edge, Weaver often
uses the language masterfully even though his grammar can be
frightful.

In the Buford–Johnson dispute Weaver told *Baltimore Morning Sun's* Jim Elliot, "I never said any pitcher, including Johnson,
threw at one of my players intentionally. My remark was based on
'if' any pitcher throws intentionally at a batter."

Earl then drew upon one of his favorite verbal tricks—calling
upon the Lord to uncover the truth.

"Johnson is the only person on earth who knows if he did or did
not throw intentionally at Buford. However, there is a higher
source who will come to judge sooner or later. Let Johnson say
again whether the pitch was intentional or not. If he says yes, we
will take it from there. If he denies it, as far as I'm concerned it's a
forgotten and buried issue."

Notice how Weaver had switched from a precarious spot to the offensive. The man always values words and he picks them like a veteran pitcher mixing a changeup, curve, and fastball. Just listen as he continued to muddle the Johnson–Buford affair.

"I want to say that I have a report from a personnel [sic] on the Chicago White Sox club saying he did hit Buford intentionally. But this is from someone other than Johnson on the ball club, so it is only secondhand. I said again last night I don't know if Johnson intentionally hit Buford. I'm surprised to see it in the papers. That was when I got my secondhand report, that the Chicago personnel said he did it on purpose. I feel he pitched immaturely, and just went and made an immature statement because his source of information was incompetent and unreliable."

In reference to a report that he had said, "Johnson doesn't belong in the majors," Weaver replied, "If Johnson continues to pitch the way he did Monday [when he hit Buford] he more than likely will go back to the minors."

There you have it, a public relations lesson—alias Stonewalling 101—straight from the mouth of Earl Weaver. Johnson was so overwhelmed by the verbal barrage that he never pursued the matter.

Another incident which illustrates Weaver's loyalty to Buford came late in the 1972 season. This was one of the few times that Earl has permitted his emotions to cloud his judgment.

"That was a bad year for us," said Earl. "We had won three straight pennants and Don Buford was a big reason we did. He was as important to our offense as any player I have ever had. One year, with runners on third base and less than two outs, he scored them 19 straight times. That is something you don't forget. In 1972, Buford was struggling. He was in a slump all year, hitting around .206. Still, I continued to write him on the lineup card. I kept thinking that he wasn't having a good year, that he could have a hot month and get us going. He never did. I should have benched him down the stretch because I had some kids like Don Baylor waiting for a chance. But Buford was a money player. He was the kind of guy you wanted in there in a big game. And the more he tried in 1972, the worse it got."

This points up another side of Weaver—the second guesser. Ten years later, he is still mentally kicking himself for playing Don Buford one season too long.

After batting .206 for the Birds in 1972, Buford signed a hefty three-year contract to play with the Fukuoka Lions in Japan. He was one of the first American ballplayers to continue his career in the Orient. When he retired from baseball, he was hired by the Sears and Roebuck Company.

"One thing about Donnie, he was smart," recalled Weaver. "He always wore a Sears and Roebuck Company glove. It wasn't much of a mitt. Most guys used big-name gloves like Wilson or Rawlings. But when he retired, Donnie got a job with Sears. So I guess he knew what he was doing."

Though pleased with the new job, Buford longed to return to baseball. He received a chance to go back in 1981 and is now a coach under San Francisco Manager Frank Robinson.

"Earl did a great job in 1968," said Harry Dalton. "The Tigers were too far in front for us to catch them, but Earl made the team competitive. He woke them up and used Buford, who supplied a lot of spark. Earl was smart. When Paul Blair started to hit, he put him back in center and had Buford play some in right and left field. That first year, Earl wasn't on the umpires very much. He was still feeling his way."

Still, Weaver's mouth did create some controversy. The Birds were playing Detroit when Tiger starter Earl Wilson left the game after five innings. "What is Wilson going to do?" Weaver asked after the contest. "Quit after five innings with his club fighting for the pennant?"

Wilson said nothing that day. A month later, the two clubs met again. Wilson hurled for Detroit and beat the Orioles. He was still enraged over Weaver's previous statement.

"How long has Weaver been around to say that?" asked Wilson. "Maybe a month? It would seem to me he would have enough to worry about with his own club without worrying about ours. Beats me how he could say stuff like that about me, a guy who has been in the big leagues for eight years and is starting every fourth day. In that game I was hit in the leg with a line drive. I know I wouldn't say something like that about him if he was injured."

As it turned out, Earl Weaver would be around long after Earl Wilson had retired.

5

Genius or Brat

It was September 22, 1979. Earl Weaver paced the clubhouse. Outside, the Memorial Stadium field was drenched, thanks to a late afternoon Baltimore shower.

While many managers deny looking at the scoreboard to track other games during the pennant race, Weaver relishes it. Weaver has the best record among active skippers in the heat of a September pennant race, and that seems to help him watch the board without fearing pressure. But there is still apprehension.

"It doesn't matter how many times you go through it, the same tension is there," said Weaver. "From the day you get into first place, you want the season to end. You always have the fear of blowing it. But that's not the worst. The worst is being in second place, three games out with only two games left."

On this day, Weaver's Birds had a comfortable lead over Milwaukee. The Brewers were engaged in a contest in Minnesota. If they lost, Weaver would have the sixth championship in his 11th full year in the Majors.

Weaver walked out of his office and into the dressing room.

"We got a doubleheader with Cleveland tonight," he

screamed. "There'll be no celebrating until after the games. We got a duty to the fans to go out there a play and not have nothing to drink."

Forty-eight bottles of champagne were on ice and Weaver desperately wanted to know what was happening in Minnesota.

Three days earlier, he said, "I keep counting how many games we have left. I wish we'd play our last nine games in the next four days. Then we'd be sure of winning a few of them. And I don't want to hear any more about this magic number shit. As of 10:30 P.M. tonight, I declare there is no such thing as a magic number. You writers can use it in your stories, but I don't want to hear about it and I sure as hell ain't gonna talk about it. What I want is another one of those one-game winning streaks. If we put four or five of those one-game winning streaks in a row, that will end the race, not the miserable magic number."

At this point, the Orioles were in front by 11 games.

"No team in the history of baseball has ever blown a lead like we have this late in the season," explained Weaver. "Right now, we have a chance to do it. All of this is getting to me. I got to the park at 2:30 P.M. for an 8 P.M. game. I can't sleep. I tried taking naps. I ate breakfast twice. Then I sat around home. Finally, I decided to come to the park and get it over with."

Yes, Earl was in a frenzy before and after games. But he had been through far worse. Remember the span from 1963—67 when he either won or lost the pennant each year on the final day of the season.

"I know having a big lead is bad," said Weaver. "But I'll take it over a tight race any time. I prefer it that way for the same reason I like 6—1 or 5—0 games over one-run jobs. It makes it easier."

Carrying it one step further, this also explains why Earl opts to swing for the home run instead of giving the bunt sign. If you bunt, you usually need another hit to win. If you hit the ball over the wall, you have no other concerns.

All of this and more ran through Weaver's mind as the Orioles were on the verge of the 1979 pennant. As he talked, former *Washington Star* baseball writer Dan Shaughnessy used the telephone in Weaver's office to call the Minnesota press box.

"Earl, it's almost over," Shaughnessy said. "Minnesota is leading 6–1 in the bottom of the eighth."

"It ain't over till it's over," said Weaver, borrowing a line from Yogi Berra.

At this point Weaver left his office and went into the clubhouse. Shaughnessy remained on the phone.

"One out in the ninth," he yelled to Weaver. "Hey, Earl, guess who's the umpire behind the plate? Ron Luciano."

"Do you believe that?" asked Weaver, who had drawn a suspension earlier in the season for questioning Luciano's integrity. "What about now?"

"Base hit," said Shaughnessy, who paused for a moment. "Earl, Sixto Lezcano just homered. It's 6–3 Minnesota."

"Hang up," roared Weaver. "We're jinxing them . . . . Hang up."

Shaughnessy put the phone down.

Weaver returned to his office, pacing.

"Go ahead, call back. Find out what's happening now."

Back on the phone, Shaughnessy told the large audience that had formed in the clubhouse that Mike Marshall was the new Minnesota pitcher.

"Tell him to scuff up them baseballs like he does against us," said Orioles Pitching Coach Ray Miller.

"He walked a guy," said Shaughnessy.

"Jesus," said Weaver, leaving the room again.

"Jim Gantner just beat out a bunt single. One out and two on," said Shaughnessy.

"Don't tell me till it's over," said Weaver.

"Two out," said Shaughnessy. "Robin Yount is up."

Weaver was back in the room. "What happened?" he demanded.

"That's it," said Shaughnessy at 5:18 P.M. "Yount flew out to right."

"It's over," yelled Weaver.

In the clubhouse, players embraced. There were smiles

and tears. Earl was among the troops. He shook hands with everyone.

"Thanks for those 15 wins," Earl said to pitcher Dennis Martinez. He delivered personal messages to all the other Birds.

The Orioles went out and lost, 7–3, to Cleveland. The second game was rained out and the celebration began.

Up with the music. Out came the beer, champagne, and food.

"You haven't quit all year," screamed Weaver, holding a bottle of bubbly. "Don't quit now."

With that, players poured champagne on each other. They poured it on visitors. They poured it on themselves. They even poured a little in their mouths.

Then the parade to the showers began. Everyone was pulled under the water. People also were dunked in the whirlpool. Don Stanhouse had a stuffed gorilla in his locker and the animal was doused with beer and champagne.

"He's my friend," said Stanhouse. "He should celebrate, too."

Stanhouse then carried the animal to the whirlpool and gave it a bath. This type of activity went on for over three hours.

"It was like the time I played in the 1958 Little League World Series," said John Lowenstein. "We lost to a team from Mexico but had a big party anyhow. The only difference is that big leaguers are a little more profane than little leaguers. Both groups are pretty messy, though."

Earl only smiled. The scene brought back wonderful memories.

The T-shirts read, BALTIMORE HAS CRABS! When Earl Weaver took over as manager of the Orioles, the town had plenty of crabs and it also had the blues. The city resigned itself to being thankful for small favors, such as the existence of Cleveland, which kept Baltimore from being a national joke.

But that did not stop Baltimore from taking more shots to the head than Jerry Quarry. *Los Angeles Times* columnist Jim Murray called it, "a complicated truck stop." Baltimore is 45 miles from

Washington and 90 miles from Philadelphia. Compared to those cities, Ballmer (as the natives call it) felt like an acne-scarred step-sister. Its proximity to Washington especially gave the city an inferiority complex. Washington is the nation's capital while Ballmer isn't even the capital of Maryland. The streets are too small for a government limousine. In any case, those were the weary lines of the critics.

Baltimore is more like a town than like a city. Its streets are narrow. Some are brick. Downtown you run across old black men in horse-drawn wagons peddling fruit and vegetables. The summers are as unyielding as a sauna, and the natives spend a good deal of time on the front steps of their row houses. No one has a front lawn—just a sidewalk. It is a place of mills, factories, and shipyards. The Chesapeake Bay is its blood. It was also the home of the country's most infamous red light district. "The Block" spawned such striptease stars as Fannie Fox, who later moved down Interstate 95 and took up with Congressman Wilbur Mills.

The city has few idealists. H.L. Mencken is the town's chief man of letters. The critics say only a place like Baltimore could produce a cynic like Mencken. In fact, most of Baltimore's citizens would have a difficult time grasping Mencken's work. They are blue collar folk with dirty fingernails and damn proud of it. They were Richard Nixon's Silent Majority. To them, Mencken was good because everybody said he was, but you couldn't prove it by them. Baltimore is Earl Weaver's kind of place.

Weaver started as a working-class manager. He paid his dues. Like Rodney Dangerfield, he felt he got no respect. Baltimore was of the same disposition. That is why Memorial Stadium fans reach the lunatic fringe when Weaver goes jaw-to-jaw with an umpire or kicks dirt on home plate. He demands a fair shake and some attention from the powers that be. If they don't listen, Earl will rip up the rulebook or walk off with third base. When Weaver began managing, he continually told the press his wars with umpires were designed to earn their respect.

"Weaver expects to get the umpires' respect by the way he acts?" asked former umpire Jim Honochick in 1969. "Well, you better tell him he won't get our respect until he acts like an adult."

The umpires were baffled by Weaver's actions, but the fans

understood. Oh, he juggled the facts to suit his own purpose. Sometimes, he was just plain wrong. The fans realized all of this. But they also knew he screamed and kicked and stomped and clawed for every advantage, and they loved him for it.

In 1968, Weaver pulled the Birds to four games behind Detroit before they faded to 10½ back. In addition to Jim Palmer being out with an arm many thought was dead, Frank Robinson was hampered by, of all things, the mumps and a vision problem. He slumped to .268 and was occasionally booed. Paul Blair batted .211, perennial prospect Curt Blefary hit .200, and the team mark was an abysmal .225.

This was not a good year for baseball. The world was in turmoil with race riots, Vietnam, college demonstrations, and assassinations. The country was not in the mood for baseball. Many said the game was destined to be a dinosaur. Its slow pace was overrun by the emergence of football. Pitchers dominated the game. Oakland's .240 team batting average was tops in the American League. Half of the clubs batted less than .230. Carl Yastrzemski saved the AL the embarrassment of not having a .300 hitter. A strong finish gave Yaz a .301 mark. Long-forgotten Danny Cater was second at .290. Detroit's McLain went 31–6, and he is the last pitcher to break the 30-win barrier. Five AL hurlers had ERAs under 2.00. Bob Gibson set a National League record by compiling an unbelievable 1.12 ERA for the Cardinals.

All you need to know about baseball in 1968 is summed up by one statistic: Twenty-one percent of all the games were shutouts. Attendance in both leagues dropped; so did television ratings. Baseball had entered a new dead-ball era and it was killing the fans.

But after the season, the game expanded and went to four six-team divisions and a playoff system for the first time. Also, Marvin Miller appeared on the scene and the players made their first serious strike threat. But the game was changing. Bowie Kuhn became commissioner. The Golden Era—in more ways than one—for the players and owners was about to dawn. Weaver would be a large part of it.

It began in 1969.

The Orioles went to spring training in Miami, and Weaver was worried about his job.

"I didn't think I'd get fired in the spring or anything like that," he recalled. "But I wanted to get off on the right foot. I played my regulars a lot. I left Boog Powell, Frank and Brooks Robinson, and the rest in there until the game was won. We had a 19–5 record in the spring. I didn't want the folks back in Baltimore to think Weaver was an idiot before the season started.

"Actually, that is not the way to run spring training. You should play everyone. The final score matters little. You practice bad managing in the spring because you are making the kind of moves and substitutions you'd never even consider during the season."

"In 1969, Earl started fast and got us so far out in front of the pack no one came close," says Harry Dalton. "He was developing his system. More and more, he was relying on statistics to make decisions. He knew how to handle the veterans and how to use his bench. He is the best I have ever seen at knowing when to take out a pitcher. He was gutsy. He would rather make a move and lose than just sit by."

"Earl was in charge from the start," said Frank Robinson. "He treated everybody the same and wouldn't back off from anyone. He may never have played in the majors, but he left no doubt in your mind that he knew he was a big league manager. He never lacked confidence."

"The biggest thing Earl had going for him was he let us play ball," said Brooks Robinson. "He didn't over manage. He knew we had talent and he didn't get in the way of it. He was fiery, much more so than Hank Bauer. When you play for Earl Weaver, you never have to worry that your team will be out-managed."

Weaver's 1969 Orioles were the classic juggernaut. They won 109 games and the Eastern Division title by 19 games. For them, the pennant race was over in August. The only faltering came at the end of the season, when they dropped six of eight games.

"We were so far in front, I was telling guys to take it easy," said Weaver. "I didn't want anyone running into walls, sliding wrong, or messing up their arm for the playoffs. I used mostly rookies in the last month of the season. The record for the most wins is 111 (the 1954 Indians), and getting the record meant nothing to me at the time. Now, sometimes I think about it and I wish we had gone for it. It would be nice to have managed the most successful team in baseball history."

While Earl won far more games than he did arguments with umpires, his highly personal style went nationwide for the first time.

One incident still discussed is this:

As always, Earl was puffing on a Raleigh cigarette in the dugout. There is a rule forbidding smoking during a game. Umpire Bill Haller spotted Earl sneaking a cigarette in the dugout runway while the Orioles were playing the Twins. Haller ejected Weaver and a $200 fine from the American League office followed.

The next night, Earl walked to home plate with the lineup cards for the pre-game meeting with the umpires. Haller saw something that looked like a cigarette dangling from Earl's lips. Once again, he was thumbed. This time, it was before the first pitch.

But Earl literally had the last laugh. He took the alleged cigarette out of his mouth, peeled off some paper, showed it to the umpires and then ate it. It was candy. However, the umpires were not about to change their minds. Earl was banished.

There were several other run-ins. Many wondered about Earl's motives, and this included some of his biggest backers. Among those was *Baltimore Evening Sun* baseball writer Doug Brown, who analyzed the situation this way:

> There is probably no truth to the story that when Earl Weaver was born, he bawled not because the doctor slapped him but because when he opened one eye he thought he saw an umpire.
>
> That may be apocryphal, but a rapidly growing segment of the Oriole congregation is convinced that Weaver is a congenital umpire agitator.
>
> Fresh evidence was provided over the weekend in Minnesota. The Oriole manager was caught smoking in the dugout, was accused of making obscene gestures when apprehended and mocked the umpires by going to the plate with a taffy cigarette in his mouth.
>
> Twice during the series with the Twins he was banished. The second episode Sunday prompted umpire Frank Umont to say that Weaver "has got to change a lot of ways" before he'll win the respect of the leagues umpires.
>
> It could be argued that Weaver was not himself over the weekend, that he was worried about his wife, who was injured in an automobile accident. Even Earl would not offer that as an excuse for his behavior.
>
> It is with some reluctance and only after considerable thought that this boom is being lowered on Weaver.

It can't be overlooked that, no matter how hard he has been on umpires, he has the Orioles running away in the AL East. Further, he has color, so rare, so cherished in baseball.

Chances are some fans this week will buy tickets to (1) see for themselves what that crazy Weaver is going to do next or (2) boo him or (3) be at ringside in the event Earl punches an umpire. Next to winning, nothing sells tickets like controversy.

In short, Weaver should be the ideal manager. He runs a good game, uses his players to the best advantage and has a sense of public relations in that he is cooperative and quotable.

But smoking in the dugout, obscene gestures and continual bickering with umpires hardly qualify as a shining example for the youth of a nation who are desperately in need of shining examples to follow.

To determine the degree of censure Weaver merits one must be a mindreader. Is he harassing umpires because, in the absence of a race, he feels the daily excitement will keep his players at a fever pitch?

Or is he doing it in hopes of intimidating the umpires? It may have worked for him in the minors, but it is only alienating them up here. If the race were close and Weaver were behaving as he is now, it is unlikely that Oriole management would tolerate it.

Yes, there were some doubts about Weaver, but his success erased most of them.

Naturally, Earl didn't win 109 games by himself. He had a brilliant team. Harry Dalton pulled one of the great swaps of his career when he stuck the Astros with the disgruntled Curt Blefary and received in return Mike Cuellar, a lefthanded screwball pitcher whose swiftest offering could be caught barehanded. Cuellar won 23 games for the Birds and the Cy Young Award in 1969. He became the first of many pitchers to have the best seasons of their careers under Weaver. Jim Palmer returned from two years of arm miseries to go 16–4. Dave McNally went 20–7. Paul Blair hit a career-high 26 homers. Boog Powell crushed 37 homers good for 121 RBI. Frank Robinson rebounded from several minor injuries in 1968 to bat .300 with 32 HR and 100 RBI. Brooks Robinson was magnificent at third and drove in 84 runs. Even the anemic-hitting Mark Belanger batted a career-high .287. Belanger, Brooks Robinson, Blair, and second baseman Dave Johnson all were Gold Glove winners.

The Orioles were said to be so loaded that Weaver received virtually no consideration for Manager of the Year honors. That award went to Billy Martin of the Twins. Minnesota won the American League West, but dropped three straight to the Birds in

the first American League playoff series. If you think Weaver is
frantic during the regular season, the playoffs come very close to
pushing him over the edge.

"The playoffs are simply the worst," he says. "You play 162
games all year and end up with the best record in the American
League. Then you have to win a best-of-five series with a Western
[Division] club to get into the World Series. It can drive you nuts.
All that work from the beginning of spring training produces a
great season, and then it all can go down the tube in the playoffs. I
know the playoffs are great for the fans, but they are hell on the
players and managers."

While the games with Minnesota were tight, the Orioles were
in control. That firm hand on events would slip in the World
Series. As the Orioles prepared to play the New York Mets . . .
let's stop right here. What were the Mets doing in the World
Series only seven years after they had been the worst team ever
assembled? Along with the rest of the world, outside of Queens,
Weaver wondered about it. A superstitious sort wary of the
powers of fate, he didn't like it one bit. Basically, the Mets were
still a miserable team. Ron Swoboda? Ed Charles? Al Weis? Rod
Gaspar? J.C. Martin? Who were these guys? After the Orioles'
4–1 opening game victory, they were good enough to kiss the
Birds off in four straight and put the final touches on their miracle
season.

"People say it was an embarrassment to lose to the Mets," said
Weaver. "They said we weren't ready, had grown lazy because of
our big lead. But we played well in the playoffs. They just pitched
better than us. That was the difference."

The Mets also seemed to have the gods on their side. Usually a
hazard to himself and the Mets pitchers, Swoboda played the
greatest defensive outfield of his life during the World Series.
Donn Clendenon acted like Hank Aaron and the Mets received
incredible pitching from Tom Seaver, Nolan Ryan, and Jerry
Koosman. Baltimore could manage only five runs in the last four
games.

There was nothing Weaver could do. He managed to get
himself ejected from Game 4, becoming only the third manager
in World Series history and the first in 35 years to be banished.

With the Mets leading 1–0, in the third, home plate umpire

Shag Crawford, a National Leaguer, walked toward the Baltimore dugout. He was shaking a finger at Weaver. Crawford had just called a strike on Mark Belanger. As Crawford strode to the Oriole bench waving his finger, Weaver strolled out of the dugout and was promptly tossed out of the game.

"I still don't know why Crawford threw me out," says Weaver. "The pitch to Belanger was low. The entire bench yelled at him. He came over. I couldn't hear him. I stepped out of the dugout and he stopped me there and said, 'You're out of the game for questioning balls and strikes.' I told him I wasn't there to argue balls and strikes, but to learn what he had said. 'Well, all you're going to hear now is you're out of the game,' he said to me. I told him he showed me up, but he also showed himself up. Then, I walked back to the dugout."

"I told him to shut his damn mouth," Crawford said. "If he didn't hear me, then his ears are as bad as he says my eyes are. He had been objecting the entire Series. Every game he came out to protest something . . . Weaver was just trying to test me. He wasn't coming out to say 'hello.' He was complaining on the second pitch of the game to Don Buford."

"Before Earl came out, Crawford yelled to the bench for Earl not to come out," said Belanger. "He wasn't arguing. He was thrown out right away."

Harry Dalton and Weaver both felt Crawford "was out to get Earl."

"Umpires are supposed to be completely unbiased and alert to today's game only," said Dalton, when informed Crawford said Weaver was complaining throughout the Series. "Crawford indicated he came into the game prejudiced . . . "

While Dalton went on and on, demanding everything short of a Congressional investigation into the matter, nothing changed. The Orioles remained losers. "And that ejection is probably the one thing in baseball which I feel really bad about," said Earl. "It really bothered my parents to see it happen on national television."

In 1970, Weaver proclaimed the Orioles, "the best team in baseball." They proved it by winning 108 games and rolling past Minnesota again in the playoffs and Cincinnati in the World Series. The following season, the Birds won 101 games and lost to

Pittsburgh in the World Series. Despite 318 victories in three seasons, Weaver was not voted Manager of the Year. Many felt he rode the crest of Baltimore's great pitching, defense, and power. The thinking was, anyone could manage Boog, Brooks, Frank & Co. to 100 triumphs.

6

Pitching and Three-Run Homers

For Earl Weaver, the worst of times is before a game.

"I go crazy sitting around and waiting for them to start," said Weaver. "I love the games, watching how good these guys play. I even know what kind of games I like. They are the ones where my pitcher is throwing a shutout and we got enough runs to make it look easy. Those close games are great for the fans, but hell on the managers."

Weaver was talking about all this and more as the Orioles prepared to go after their tenth win in a row in May of 1979. Throughout the streak, Earl wore the same T-shirt under his uniform. He used the same charmed *Flair* pen to write his lineup. He had the same Baltimore baseball writer walk to the opposing team's dressing room and write down the lineup. The writer then returned to Weaver and read the opposition's batting order to Earl, who made his own copy. Finally, Earl had Coach Frank Robinson carry the lineup card to the pre-game meeting with the umpires. When the Orioles lose, Weaver throws away his pen and breaks out a new one. He asks a different writer to get the lineup.He wears a different T-shirt and has a different coach take out the lineup card.

"We have a rotation set up between me and the coaches," said Weaver. "We all have our turn carrying the lineup card. If you win, you stay in. I remember us winning 17 straight, including two in the 1970 World Series. [Former Oriole Coach] George Staller took the lineup card out every day during the streak."

At one time, the Orioles were on a winning streak when they went to New York. Weaver could not find his lucky pen. He and two Baltimore writers spent ten minutes—much of it on their hands and knees—searching Weaver's office for the pen. When Weaver realized it was missing, he accused Yankee Owner George Steinbrenner of having someone break into the office and steal his pen. "I wouldn't put it past George," Weaver said, smiling.

Weaver fills those empty hours prior to a contest with games of his own. He plays home run derby with one of the Baltimore writers. Every day, a draft is held. Weaver picks first. Next, the writer chooses, then Earl. Each man selects three players he thinks have the best chance of hitting homers that day. If Weaver's players homer twice and the writers once, the score is 2–1 and the writer pays Earl a dollar. If the writer's team hits two homers and Weaver's is blanked, the score is 2–0 and Earl gives the scribe two dollars.

Like everything else he does, Earl wins more than he loses. Often, he collects on players like Kiko Garcia, Rick Dempsey, or Rich Dauer. He has the knack of knowing when their chances to connect are best. Garcia said Weaver once mentioned to him before a game that he had tabbed Kiko in the home run derby. Garcia homered.

But most of Earl's pre-game time is spent in the dugout. Usually, he is surrounded by writers. He asks that no one be directly in front of him, so he can watch batting practice and still answer questions. On the day of the nine-game winning streak, Earl made it clear he believes in luck. But he has no use for momentum.

"Ain't no such thing as momentum," he said. "That's all

psychological. So we won nine straight. That is nine one-game winning streaks. All of a sudden, everybody is writing about momentum. They make everything psychological. There's nothing psychological about this game. So we've won nine in a row. We are feeling good. Then, Tommy John goes out and shoves the bat right up our ass. He's a great pitcher. He can do it and he beats us, 1–0. Then what happened to all that momentum? What happened to the streak? The smartest guy who ever lived said you play them one at a time. That is how you win nine in a row. You win nine in a row one day at a time. You lose games the same way. I don't think there is much of a carryover from one game to the next. Now, players get hot. But what happens if a hot hitter faces a hot pitcher? Who has the momentum?"

The Orioles did not win that tenth straight game. They were beaten, 8–5, by Oakland. When the game was over, Weaver was in his office with a plate of franks and beans in front of him. Like most baseball managers, his post-game press conferences do not stop him from eating. His sentences were punctuated with swallows of beans and the words came out between bites into hot dogs. No matter what the score, Weaver consumes food after games as if this meal were to be his last.

"You heard of a game where everybody chips in," Weaver asked. "Tonight, nobody chipped in. What we need to do tomorrow is to start another one of them one-game winning streaks. Maybe after nine days, we'll have another nine-gamer going."

The Orioles did begin another of Earl's "one-game winning streaks." This one-game winning streak lasted six games, giving the Birds 15 victories in 16 games. Don Stanhouse was a key figure in that May rise to first place, a spot Baltimore would not relinquish that season.

"I don't know what I did to have God send Stanhouse to punish me," Weaver was saying after one of the victories. "I call the guy full pack, because that's how many cigarettes I smoke while he's in there. I can't sit still while he pitches. I keep walking back and forth, up and down the dugout runway. I stand in a lucky spot. He takes forever to throw the ball. He walks guys. I don't know how he gets anyone out sometimes. But he gets the save. Scare and a save Stanhouse is what he is."

A typical Stanhouse performance was April 25, 1979. He entered the game with the Orioles in front, 5–2, in the seventh. He put down the Angels in order until the ninth. Then, he walked two men before retiring Brian Downing to win the game. When Downing came to bat, representing the tying run, Weaver was in the dugout runway. He could not see the game. He was puffing on a Raleigh and moaning about Stanhouse.

"Not again, not again," Weaver kept repeating until Stanhouse fanned Downing to end the contest.

"Why does Stanhouse torment me," Weaver repeated after the game. "Why can't he be like everyone else and throw the ball over? He is 6–1 with 12 saves and 33 walks in 44 innings. Could you imagine him as a starter? He'd probably throw a shutout, leave 18 men on base, walk about 14, and the game would take about six hours and 20 minutes. Maybe I shouldn't complain. He does the job. Maybe he wouldn't be as good if he were like everyone else."

To Weaver's credit, he never did try to change Stanhouse. You don't fiddle with success. Instead, Earl made sure he had on the right T-shirt, stood in the proper spot of the dugout runway, and puffed away at a Raleigh. If you want to keep those one-game winning streaks going, you can't leave anything to chance.

Earl Weaver contends baseball is a simple game.

"Winning comes down to two things; pitching and three-run homers," Weaver tells anyone who requests a success formula. "I love home runs. They are instant runs. You can have a couple guys on base and with one swing of the bat, you've got three runs. Any jerk knows when to steal or bunt, but that doesn't win many games over the long haul. Pitching and home runs do. We keep winning because our pitchers hold the other team down until one of our guys hits the ball out of the park."

A team without power irks Weaver. "Nothing but a bunch of lead-off men," he calls those clubs in disdain.

Weaver also disdains the sacrifice bunt.

"In most cases, it is nothing but a wasted out," says Weaver. "I would rather have a man on first with no outs than a runner at second with one out. By bunting, you give up one of your chances to hit a homer or drive a runner in with an extra-base hit. You take away a big inning."

Weaver will bunt if the game is tied in the late innings or if Mark Belanger is the batter. Belanger seldom hits, and when he does it is usually a single. He is also an expert bunter.

In Weaver's mind the bunt is bad, but the hit-and-run play is worse.

"Now there is stupidity," says Weaver. "In the hit-and-run, you have a guy running to second, but he is not going full speed like he would if he were stealing. You make the batter swing at any pitch, no matter where it is. It puts everyone on the defensive. If I want that runner on second base, I'll have him steal or bunt him over. I really think it is the worst play in baseball."

That brings us back to home runs and pitching.

In the minor leagues, most young players are told not to think about home runs. Swing naturally and homers will come is the favorite phrase of coaches.

"That's bullshit," says Weaver. "I remember when Don Baylor came up from Rochester. He is a big guy, and he is hitting the ball up the middle, going for singles. What is that? We used to yell at him to stand near the plate and pull the ball. Hit it down the line, it is closer to the stands that way. He is a big guy, he should hit home runs. But he kept telling us he was good for only 10–15 a year. He never became a full-fledged power hitter until he went to the Angels. Then, he started doing the things we had been telling him for five years."

"Earl is the first manager I have run into who tells you to hit homers," said Oriole outfielder Gary Roenicke. "Most managers don't want you to even think about homers because they feel it will mess up your swing."

In the late 1970s, Weaver recalled Andres Mora from Rochester over Roenicke. Roenicke was batting .300, Mora .240.

"Earl likes those homers," said Frank Robinson, who was Roenicke's manager in Rochester. "I told Gary that is why Earl promoted Mora. Then, Roenicke asked me what he had to do to hit the ball out."

Robinson moved Roenicke's batting stance near home plate and told the 6–3, 200-pounder to attack the ball. In 1979 it worked and he smashed 25 homers in 376 at bats. His power has gradually disappeared since then, however.

Weaver readily admits home runs are meaningless without pitching. Great arms have always been the core of the Orioles. They have been present for so long there is a tendency to take them for granted.

"There is a reason Earl always has good pitching," said George Bamberger. "Earl and Billy Martin know how to handle pitching. They have more patience than most managers. They don't run to the bullpen when the score is 2–1 in the seventh inning. Earl has great confidence in his starters and the pitchers feel the same way toward him. That's why they don't look over their shoulders to the dugout or bullpen when they get into a jam. Martin and Earl make their pitchers proud of complete games. It's what makes a pitcher great. Besides, who wants a pitcher who is always looking over his shoulder for help."

"Earl has the great instinct of when to remove a pitcher," said Blue Jays General Manager Pat Gillick. "That is something you don't learn. By the time Earl walks to the mound, he already knows whether he will take a pitcher out or leave him in. He won't let the pitcher change his mind. Earl also knows how to treat his bullpen. He won't ask you to warm up unless there is a good chance you'll get into the game. When I played for him, I'd say there was a 90% possibility of getting in a game when he asked you to warm up. That is important because a lot of managers make guys get up and throw and then sit down 3 or 4 times a game. After awhile, pitchers don't take those managers seriously."

The consensus about Weaver is that he treats his team the best when it is losing.

"Earl is at his best when things are worst," said Orioles Pitching Coach Ray Miller. "He takes the heat and keeps the press off our backs. But when we're hot, he is just the opposite. He is on everybody all the time. He knows we're going well and he doesn't want us to let down."

Miller became the Orioles' Pitching Coach in 1978, replacing Bamberger, who was named manager by the Brewers. Many said Bamberger was the salient reason for the superb Baltimore pitching and it would falter after his departure. Miller found him-

self in one of the most pressurized situations ever faced by a
coach.

"In 1978, we opened the season with three games in Milwaukee and gave up 40 runs and threw seven wild pitches," said
Miller. "Everybody was worrying about how I felt taking over for
Bamberger and then having a disaster like that. Publicly, Earl
kept the critics off me."

But that first year was not easy for Miller. He and Weaver were
still learning about each other.

"Back then, Earl sometimes got to me," said Miller. "It seemed
no matter how good we pitched, it wasn't good enough because
we weren't hitting or winning. He'd get on me, asking me why a
pitcher threw a certain pitch in the seventh inning. Or he'd ask
me why the guy on the mound walked a batter when it was
obvious he didn't want to walk the guy. His control was just off.
Sometimes, I'd have to remind Earl that it was the seventh inning
and the pitcher had given up only three hits, so he couldn't be
doing too badly."

Miller is the Oriole who is closest to Weaver in the dugout.

"He talks through the entire game," said Miller. "He'll keep
yelling at the umpire. Where was that pitch? Inside? Outside? In
the second inning, he usually checks his statistics. By the fourth,
he'll say something to me like Terry Crowley is the guy who wins
the game. It will come down to Crowley and a certain relief
pitcher in the eighth inning. He is four innings ahead of everyone
else and his predictions are right a lot of the time."

The way Weaver employs reserves like Crowley has received a
lot of attention.

"You got to have guys on the bench who can go up and get the
hit to win the game," said Weaver. "We always have good depth.
Our depth is deep depth."

Deep depth.

Earl says it over and over. Then, he pulls out this phrase, "We
have a lot of guys who have a lot to get a lot out of." Ever since he
was calling the shots in Fitzgerald, Georgia, Weaver has been
getting more out of his players than most managers do.

"I hear about Earl's great bench and I wonder," said Indians
General Manager Phil Seghi. "But I look at the guys he
has—Benny Ayala, Dan Graham, John Lowenstein, Terry
Crowley, Lenn Sakata, and Jose Morales—and it is not bad, but

nothing great, either. Ayala was dumped by the Mets and Cardinals. Atlanta released Crowley. The Twins gave up on Graham and Sakata could not stick with the Brewers. Lowenstein knocked around for years. But all those guys play like stars when Earl uses them. They become different ballplayers when they go to Baltimore, and the reason has to be Weaver."

"My real work is done before the season," explains Weaver. "It happens in the winter when a manager sits down with the general manager and talks about next season. It is your job to convince the GM what kind of players you need to win. It is his job to trade for those guys. Before you make any deal you should make up a roster with the players you are trading for and without the guys you give up. Then you should compare that roster with your original one and see which is better. Then comes spring training, that is the hardest part. There you have to get the fundamentals worked out and find the best 25 guys who will win the most games."

Players say Weaver has the most organized spring training camp in baseball. Very little time is spent standing around. The workouts are quick and brisk, and there is a plethora of drills.

"Earl delegates authority very well," said George Bamberger. "He gives every coach something to do. They do most of the teaching. Earl coordinates everything. He is a great man to coach under because he backs you 100%. Weaver does little if any actual teaching."

In the spring of 1979, Weaver's primary concern was the outfield. The preceding season, it had been a disaster. Outfielders stood and stared at each other as balls dropped between them. Other times, they collided pursuing routine fly balls. In the dugout, Earl would do imitations of Carlos Lopez circling under a fly ball and waving the other outfielders off. Then Weaver would lunge forward and dive to the ground in Lopez' fashion.

"That's why I made Frank Robinson Outfield Coach and Communication Director," said Weaver. "It is Frank's job to keep these guys from running into each other and get them to call for the ball."

At the first team meeting, Weaver looked on as Robinson held out a mitt and said, "Gentlemen, this is a glove."

"I told Frank to go right back to the basics," said Weaver. "He did, and it worked. In 1979, we had no trouble in the outfield."

One of Weaver's favorite lines is, "A manager wins games in the winter and spring by the way he picks his team. He tries not to lose them in July." A week into spring training, and Weaver's voice is usually nothing more than a rasp, like the sound of tires on gravel.

"I thought of giving instructions over the public address system," said Weaver. "One year, I came out on the field with a bullhorn, but no one listened. They were laughing too hard."

If the Orioles have won a championship the season before, Weaver starts warning of complacency on the first day of spring training. "I don't want to hear any shit about last year's 100 wins," he tells the team. "The toughest thing to do is to win again. You've forgotten how cold and miserable it can be playing in Detroit, Cleveland, or Milwaukee when it's 41 degrees in April or May. That's a big change from the World Series. I don't want to hear anything about last year. You've got to do it all over again."

Weaver spends every spring day pondering his final roster. Usually, 20–22 of the 25 spots are set, but he maintains the decision made on those last 3–5 players often are the difference between first and second place.

"Most teams pick the best 25 players at the end of spring," said Frank Robinson. "Not Earl. He takes everything into consideration. A guy may be a good athlete, but how will he perform off the bench. Can he fill the role the team needs. Weaver looks to see who can be a good pinch runner, or a pinch hitter, or a long reliever. Those guys win games and you need people suited to those jobs. Earl puts those things together better than anyone else because he probably is the best judge of talent in baseball."

"The Orioles don't have a wasted player on their roster," said Harry Dalton. "From their No. 1 to their No. 25 player, they can beat you. It is always like that with Earl."

"I like to have veterans on the bench," says Weaver. "Sometimes, a kid may be a better player, but he is not ready to sit for a long period of time and then hit. Veterans know how to keep themselves in shape. Guys like Terry Crowley do that very well."

"Earl prides himself in having the right hitter facing the right pitcher," said Crowley. "That sometimes means you get four hits and are on the bench the next day because you have bad statistics against a pitcher. But Earl uses everyone and keeps them sharp. That is why Pat Kelly struggled when he went from the Orioles to

Cleveland. The Indians didn't use him enough or in the right spots."

"I have a very simple system for deciding who plays each day," said Weaver. "I have a list of how each of our hitters faired against every pitcher. To decide who starts, I just write down the names of the guys who have the most success against that day's pitcher. I don't use that for everyone in the lineup [Eddie Murray and Ken Singleton play all the time], but it applies to most guys. You need about 20 at bats to get the real trend of a hitter against a pitcher, but if one of your hitters is 2-for-4 and no one else has done anything against the pitcher, you got to go with the 2-for-4 guy. Ideally, you try to get as many guys batting .300 against a pitcher as you can in the lineup. You'd be surprised how bad a lifetime .300 hitter looks when he is facing a pitcher he is batting .095 against. If I don't have any data on how a hitter does against a specific pitcher, I check to see how he does against the team we are facing."

Here are some examples of Earl's statistics and their use:

Mark Belanger is 9-for-14 against Jim Kern. Logic would dictate a weak hitter like Belanger would have no chance against a fastball pitcher like Kern. The numbers tell a different story. In 1979, Weaver sent Belanger to pinch hit against Kern. It was one of the few times in his career Belanger was used as a pinch hitter. Belanger lined a single. By the way, Belanger is also 7-for-17 vs. flamethrower Rich Gossage.

Early in Weaver's reign, the Orioles did not have detailed records. When they finally were put together, Weaver discovered Boog Powell was 1-for-61 against Mickey Lolich. Powell never again batted against Lolich while he was a member of the Orioles.

There was a game in 1980 when the Tigers brought in Dave Rozema from the bullpen. Benny Ayala was the batter. Weaver checked his statistics against Rozema and ordered Ayala back to the bench. The call went to Pat Kelly.

"Kelly was 5-for-7 with three homers against Rozema," said Weaver after the game. "Now, he is 6-for-8 with four homers. It's like Monopoly. The object is to get some hotels on Park Place and stay off the utilities. Now our stats go all the way back to 1968."

Weaver's hitting statistics are kept on 8 × 11 ½ inch sheets. His pitching records—how to attack opposing hitters and how those hitters have performed against each Baltimore pitcher—are kept in a file box. Every American League batter can be found on an index card. If the batter is released or traded, even to the National League, his card is not thrown out. It is put in another file where Earl can consult it if the player returns to the American League.

. The cards are cold, faceless. Weaver tries to treat his players the same way.

"I don't think a manager can be their friend," says Weaver. "You are the one who sets the rules. You are the one who tells them they are benched or traded. You have to fire them, look them square in the eye and tell them they're through. In many ways, you decide the worst things in their baseball careers. And you have to do it. You must keep the best 25 players on your team in order to protect your job."

But Weaver does consider a player's personality.

"I never jump on a guy for something until I hear his explanation," says Earl. "Sometimes, it may seem logical to a player and stupid to everyone else, then you can't come down hard on the guy. You have to know your players, but you can't be their friend."

Weaver does strive to create a certain mood in the clubhouse.

"I like for the guys to talk about baseball," says Weaver. "I want the young players to hear the veterans say the right things. I like a smart team, one with its head in the game. I want my players to think any one of them can be Mr. September and Mr. October for us, the guy who comes through down the stretch. In any year, we got 6–7 guys who can do it. We just have to find out who they are and they have to believe that they can do it."

When the Orioles are winning, there are few workouts. The team spends off days at home. When they lose, everybody is at the stadium every day.

"I like it to be hard when they lose," said Weaver. "I want it to be harder for them to lose than to win."

The defeats also haunt Weaver. While he is generally pleasant around his players during these periods, he stays up late, second-guessing himself.

"I wonder if I should stick with a guy who hasn't had a hit in 4–5 games," said Weaver. "I think, maybe I should sit him down.

Then, I think tomorrow might be the day he snaps out of it. I wonder if I went to the bullpen too soon or not soon enough. When you lose, all these things and more run through your mind."

But Weaver has unyielding faith in his veterans. Once you have proven your worth to Earl, his patience can seem endless.

"I tell a player, 'This is your job, show me you can do it,'" explains Weaver. When they do, Earl is their staunchest supporter. In the case of some players, such as Elrod Hendricks and Tom Shopay, he wanted to keep them after their careers clearly were over.

"The hardest thing to figure is if a guy is having an off-season or if he's done," said Weaver. "If a guy has done it for you before, you tend to think he is in a slump and when he comes out of it, he'll help you again. If you don't know the player and he has some age, you think he's washed up. You can get burned. In 1979, Ken Singleton started slow. Kenny had always hit for me before, so I kept him in the lineup. Eventually, he hit. In 1972, Donnie Buford started slow. He batted .290 the year before, and I thought he'd get started again. He never did."

Earl learned patience from watching his club. The Orioles usually fall flat in April. They close quickly in September.

"Every year, I go through the same thing, writers asking me why we start slow," said Weaver. "But what's a slow start? One game? Ten games? Fifty games? You tell me what a start is and I'll tell you how we are starting. If it is the month of April, we usually don't start too good. If it is the first 50 games, by then we ain't bad. It's all relative."

And it is all confusing, which is exactly the way Weaver wants it. He does not want the writers to dwell on the Orioles' annual early-season problems. He knows they will end, and he feels the writers should be aware of it, too. Besides, there is no need for his players to read about their dismal start every day. That does not help morale.

Weaver also has led the media away from an uncomfortable topic in other ways. In 1978, the Birds were drilled, 24–10, in Toronto. Losing by 14 runs—"only two touchdowns," said Weaver—was bad. Having the hapless Blue Jays do the smashing was even worse.

Jerry Wachter

Jerry Wachter

In most disputes between manager and umpire, the arbiter wins. Here, Earl Weaver, the most feared manager in the big leagues, states his point in typical fashion, then gives the ump the heave-ho sign—probably just before heading for the showers.

Jerry Wachter

Orioles superstars, pitcher Jim Palmer and, below, former third baseman Brooks Robinson. "See this head of gray hair?" Weaver once asked. "Every one of them belongs to Jim Palmer." "You know the ultimate test for a Timex watch?" Palmer likes to ask. "It is taping it to Earl's tongue."

Tadder/Baltimore

Tadder/Baltimore

Frank Robinson, another Orioles great, who says of Weaver, "He probably is the best judge of talent in baseball." Below, Rick Dempsey and Doug DeCinces.

Jerry Wachter

Jerry Wachter

Jerry Wachter

From the left, above, Al Bumbry, Terry Crowley and Steve Stone. Below, Don Buford.

Jerry Wachter

SUNPAPERS/J. Pat Carter

In the 1979 World Series, Mark Belanger slides into second base against Tim Foli of the Pirates and, below, Garcia gets Madlock at second and fires to first.

SUNPAPERS/J. Pat Carter

Jerry Wachter

A 1979 World Series game at Pittsburgh, above, and a night game at Baltimore.

Jerry Wachter

Jerry Wachter

Orioles executives Hank Peters, the general manager, above, and Jim McLaughlin, former farm system director. McLaughlin gave Earl Weaver his first job in the Baltimore organization as manager of the Class D team in Fitzgerald, Georgia.

Tadder/Baltimore

Tadder/Baltimore

Harry Dalton, former Orioles general manager, who brought Earl
Weaver up from the minors to manage the Baltimore team. Below,
Jim Russo, chief scout for the Orioles, who says of Weaver's minor
league abilities even in 1954, "He seemed to have the talent to ignite
players and create excitement."

Tadder/Baltimore

"The amazing thing about that game is, I thought it would never end," said Weaver. "After five innings and seven pitchers, we had given up all 24 runs." That's when Earl swung into action.

"After 24 runs, I got the impression my pitchers didn't have it," said Weaver. "I had an obligation to the fans of Toronto to get this one over as soon as possible. Larry Harlow and Elrod Hendricks were our best batting practice pitchers at the time. Hell, we've clocked Harlow at 93 mph. He pitched in the minors so I brought him in."

First, Weaver checked his rulebook.

"In the minors, there is a rule that the only people allowed to pitch must be designated pitchers," said Weaver. "There ain't no rule like that in the majors."

Weaver told umpire Steve Palermo he planned to use Harlow on the mound. Palermo said he thought it was illegal. Then he realized Earl was right and Harlow was ushered in.

"Harlow was like the rest of the pitchers," said Weaver. "He got a guy out and then started walking people. So I switched to Elrod."

Hendricks blanked the Blue Jays on one hit over 2⅓ innings. He did it by lobbing the ball down the middle. Apparently exhausted from scoring two dozen runs, the Blue Jays went out weakly. "If it weren't for Elrod, we'd still be playing that damn game in Toronto," said Weaver.

Meanwhile, Toronto President Peter Bavasi called American League President Lee MacPhail and complained that Weaver was "making a travesty of the game."

"If MacPhail tries to do anything or fine me, I'll have this case tried in civil court," proclaimed Weaver. "I'll present the case to a jury." MacPhail said Earl was within his rights to pitch whomever he wanted on his 25-man roster. After the game, Hendricks became a cult hero. He received a barrage of telephone calls, including one from [then Yankee Manager] Billy Martin, saying New York was seeking some healthy arms. A number of Baltimore fans called the Orioles, suggesting Hendricks receive a raise. At 37, Hendricks was thrust into the national spotlight for the first time.

Earl had several things in mind when he employed Hendricks and Harlow as pitchers. First, the slaughter was the first game of a doubleheader, and he wanted to salvage his bullpen for the second game, which the Birds also dropped. Second, he wanted to make the best of a depressing evening. He knew everyone would be talking about Hendricks' pitching rather than about the play by the Orioles. It was a face-saving measure. Earl is never afraid to muddle a subject. Around the clubhouse, it is known as the Paul Blair or Brooks Robinson story maneuver. Former Baltimore Coach Jim Frey called it that, and he used it the most.

"Whenever anyone asks me something I don't want to talk about, I tell a story about Blair or Brooks," said Frey. "For example, somebody will ask me about one of our players who messed up in the outfield. I will say he is struggling, just like Paul Blair did. But I remember Paul coming around very quickly and then there was this game in Cleveland where he made this great diving catch and nobody could believe it . . . I use this a lot at banquets and by the time I'm finished, everybody remembers what a great player Blair was and they're telling Paul Blair stories, too."

While Weaver does not talk about Blair or Brooks to confuse writers, he will bring up Mark Belanger. If you ask Weaver about an Oriole infielder who is making errors, Earl swiftly reminds you Belanger booted 45 balls in his first two seasons with Baltimore. He needs to say no more . . . if Belanger used to botch grounders, it could happen to anyone.

"Earl is always thinking," says Harry Dalton. "He has a very original mind and he is open to new ideas."

Because of Weaver, the Orioles were the first team to make use of the radar gun. Weaver pays more attention to the readings than does any other manager.

"We have a guy behind the plate every game with the gun," said Weaver. "He clocks the speed of every pitch, just like the cops clock the speed of a car. Then the guy behind the plate calls in his reading on a walkie-talkie to one of our coaches in the dugout. The information is useful. For example, if Dennis Martinez was throwing his fastball at 90 mph early in the game and is down to 86 mph in the seventh, you know he is getting tired even if he doesn't look it. This way, no opposing pitcher is sneaky fast.

We tell our hitters exactly how hard the pitcher is throwing, so they know what to expect."

"Earl can get on your nerves with the radar gun," Al Bumbry has said. "I remember when we were facing Nolan Ryan and he kept saying that pitch was 96 mph and another was 94 mph. We know Ryan throws hard."

"The radar gun does not show everything," said Weaver. "It won't tell if a ball sails or moves. Jim Palmer will fool you. He'll be throwing 82–84 mph, until he gets a guy on third base. Then he'll throw 88 mph. But it's a great thing for scouting."

Of course, the radar gun will only indicate that a Tommy John sinker is 72 mph. "John don't have to throw them gravity balls fast," says Weaver.

The average major league fastball is 84 mph. Jim Kern, Rich Gossage and Nolan Ryan are in the 96 mph range. A twenty-game winner in 1980, Scott McGregor averages 82 mph. Ross Grimsley's slowest changeup is 44 mph. Once Weaver held the gun on Blair as he walked to the dugout. Blair was moving 4 mph.

Earl also has some pet tricks with his lineup. In September of 1975, Weaver penciled Royale Stillman into the leadoff spot as the Orioles' shortstop. Stillman was an outfielder.

"I had no intention of using Stillman at short," said Weaver. "I used this ploy only on the road. Stillman would be our leadoff batter in the top of the first. After he batted, Mark Belanger would go in as the shortstop."

Stillman went 4-for-9 in that spot.

Another of Weaver's tactics concerns the designated hitter. In a game late in 1980 Earl made pitcher Steve Stone his designated hitter. Interesting, in as much as the Orioles were playing in Detroit and Stone was 200 miles away in Toronto, preparing to start the next day against the Blue Jays.

Earl had received a fan letter suggesting he use a pitcher as DH. When the pitcher is due to bat, the fan advised, Earl should instead send up a pinch hitter for him. That batter would serve as the DH for the rest of the game.

"In 1980, we platooned our DH," said Weaver. "Lee May played against left-handed pitchers while Terry Crowley or Pat Kelly played against righties." What prompted all this was a game with the Tigers. May was batting fifth because he had impressive stats against Milt Wilcox. By the time May was due up in the first, Wilcox had been knocked out of the game and replaced by a pitcher who handled May easily. Weaver wanted to bat for May, but that would have meant wasting a player.

"That is when I thought back to the letter," said Weaver. "The fan didn't sign his name, but he said we should have the pitcher bat second as the DH. Then, when Al Bumbry got on, we could have a pitcher bunt him to second. You know how they love to bunt in Baltimore and how I hate it. Later in the game, the fan said we could use a pinch hitter. I thought, why not put the pitcher in there and then come up with the appropriate hitter for the situation. That way, you avoid a problem like we had with May in Detroit."

For the last month of 1980, Stone or one of the other Oriole pitchers usually appeared in the lineup as the DH. When it was their turn to bat, Earl looked to his bench for a hitter.

The American League office was not thrilled with Earl's ingenuity, and before the 1981 season a rule was passed that a DH must bat at least once unless the opposing club has changed its pitcher. Called the "Weaver Rule," it ended Stone's career as a DH.

At times Earl has been embarrassed by his own tactics. Baseball people insist 1977 was Weaver's finest managing job, but it was also the year of his two greatest blunders. They both happened in the last week of May, and Earl ended up with so much egg on his face he had to call a team meeting to apologize.

In one game, he ordered Scott McGregor to intentionally walk Jim Essian. It seemed like a reasonable idea. Essian was a right-handed batter. Lefty Ralph Garr was on deck and McGregor is a southpaw pitcher. But there was one hitch. The bases were loaded when Essian stepped to the plate. Earl was about to walk in a run. Later that year, when the Orioles were playing the Twins, Weaver ordered Mike Flanagan to walk Dan Ford. On the surface that also seemed okay, except that Earl thought Ford was Larry Hisle. Hisle was the batter after Ford.

Jim Palmer explained that the snafus could be traced to Weaver's eyesight and emotion. Palmer says Weaver sometimes becomes so excited it clouds his thinking. Also, Earl wears glasses, but not in the dugout. He could not see who was batting or who was on base. Brooks Robinson suggests Weaver fell into the trap of thinking too far ahead. His mind was three innings in front of what was taking place.

"I'm entitled to my mistakes," said Weaver. "I made two in ten years and they came together."

Certainly those mistakes were exceptions. Weaver had not pulled anything so foolhardy before, nor has he since. And in 1977, he was voted Manager of the Year.

"You can count on both hands the mistakes Earl has made during his career." says Harry Dalton. "He is not only solid, he has adapted well. He has won with power teams. He won with teams that hit singles and stole bases. His players have come and gone and kids have taken their places and Earl showed them the way. Of course he has had talent playing for him, but he has gotten the most out of it. That is the real tribute to his success."

"I work for the Orioles, so people say I have a biased attitude, but you have to agree that Earl is the best manager around," said Baltimore Scout Jim Russo. "He is not a tricky manager. He loves the three-run homer. He lives and dies with it. He doesn't even have a hit and run sign. He doesn't like to bunt because, as he says, it is easier to score a runner from first base with no outs than from second with one out. Among managers, only Gene Mauch knows the rules as well as Earl. Weaver says he respects umpires and he really means it. But when they make a mistake, he thinks that jumping on them will get him more respect. With some umpires, it works. Others just stick it to us at the next opportunity. Sometimes, I wish he'd bunt more and maybe argue with umpires less, but those are minor things. He runs a game better than anyone. He won't get backed into a corner where he is out of pinch hitters. He holds no grudges. He has shoved Doug De-Cinces and Bobby Grich up against walls in arguments and had them back in the lineup the next day. The bottom line is winning and no one has won more than Earl."

While baseball executives are almost unanimous in their praise of Weaver, opposing managers have ambivalent feelings toward him. Almost all respect him. Some are jealous of his success. Some are afraid of him. Many wish they were in his dugout with the Baltimore pitching staff and farm system behind them. Some, like Sparky Anderson, can't find enough ways to compliment him.

"I love to manage against Earl," said Anderson. "If I were an owner, I'd hire Earl as my manager and stay out of his way. I've always said managers don't win anything, but I'll guarantee you one thing, if somebody else was managing the Orioles they would not have done quite as well. They've had good players, but not the best. But they know how to play. They're uncanny. They know how to kill you when you're dying. They know how to put the bullet between your eyes. They don't beat themselves. They let a lot of other teams play stupid and then they jump in for the kill. What they've done, they have done as a team. They have been taught well by Earl and they learned how to win."

Billy Martin has a different opinion of Weaver. The two men have engaged in an on-and-off feud since 1968. It is another example of clashing egos. According to Martin, it began when Weaver was coaching first base for the Orioles in 1968. Martin was the third base coach for the Minnesota Twins. He sent a runner home on a wild pitch, but the Minnesota player was tagged out.

"Weaver was screaming like a madman, 'Nice going, Martin.' I got so mad at him I challenged him on the spot. He backed down," Martin was widely quoted as saying.

By 1969 Martin had become the Twins' manager. He was fired the following season. In 1970, Weaver said the Twins had been really hustling under new manager Bill Rigney, who replaced Martin. The implication was Martin had not inspired his team. "He went out of his way to get me with a crack like that," said Martin. "I was out of baseball, just fired after winning a division title. Now when I'm out of the game, that little flathead comes out with a remark like that. Mark my words, I'm going to get him and I'm going to hurt him. I don't care if there is a ring of five cops around him."

Martin and Weaver never have slugged it out. In fact, Earl let Billy's 1970 threat pass. But the two men have been fiercely competitive. Publicly, they usually are diplomatic. "I like Earl personally," Martin has said several times. "The feud was created by the newspaper guys to help sell tickets. I said I would get him, but that was in the heat of anger. He had taken a cheap shot at me after I got fired by the Twins. But there is nothing but respect between us."

In 1976, the truce broke down. Martin was managing the Yankees. Lou Piniella was playing for New York, and he was especially galled by Earl's propensity to shout "tough luck" at an opposing hitter who lined out, or to scream "curveball" as the Oriole pitcher was about to throw.

"It was messing up my concentration," said Piniella. Piniella had played under Weaver at Elmira. He says he asked Weaver not to scream at him while he was batting. In this particular game, Weaver was hollering "Don't hit a homer" as Piniella was batting. After making an out, Piniella walked within five feet of Weaver and the Orioles dugout before another Yankee player stopped him.

"When I went over there, Earl said he wouldn't do it anymore," said Piniella. "If he does, he'll get a good kick in the butt."

Martin then went to bat for Piniella. "If a guy challenges me like Piniella did, I've the guts to come out and handle it," said Martin. "But Earl hid behind the bat rack like a little boy. He backed off like a woman. Lou would eat him up, but I didn't want to let Lou beat up on a little midget like that."

For several years after the incident, Martin would refer to Weaver as "that little midget."

"I'd rather be small of stature than a mental midget," was Weaver's standard retort.

Recently, Martin and Weaver have gone out of their way to compliment each other. Writers covering both men say this has taken the fun out of one of the game's best battle of wits. And Earl has verbally sparred with Yankee Owner George Steinbrenner. On September 29, 1980, the Orioles trailed the first-place Yankees by 3 ½ games with five left to play. That is when Weaver tried to play psychological games with New York.

"If the Yankees lose it, George Steinbrenner will build a boat and go to the middle of the Atlantic Ocean and pull the plug," said Weaver. "The Yankees are the *Titanic* and Steinbrenner is the captain. If the Yankees blow this one, it could be the biggest fold since the 1964 Phillies lost ten in a row down the stretch."

"Tell Earl Weaver he can kiss my grits," said Steinbrenner. "We're not going to fold. I'll tell you who folded. The Orioles did in the 1979 World Series. They were up 3–1 and lost. In 1980, they got within a half game of us but couldn't pass us. They looked us in the eye and couldn't catch us. We are like a great thoroughbred. Weaver is trying to take the pressure off himself and put it on us. He is using the wrong psychology."

"George knows what I'm talking about," said Weaver. "We can't choke. But they can. I know what it is like to be in their spot. Sometimes you feel like you're not going to win another game. You don't want to be remembered as the one team who could not win that last game to take the pennant."

For all the talk, the end was a fizzle. The Yankees rolled on during the last week of 1980, recording 103 victories. The Orioles finished a strong second with 100 wins. But the exchange further enhanced Steinbrenner's respect for Earl.

"He and Billy Martin are the best managers," said Steinbrenner. "Earl is always on top of things. The man is intelligent. He scares the umpires."

It is obvious Steinbrenner would hire Weaver at the wink of an eye if Earl ever left Baltimore. But that is highly unlikely. If Los Angeles Manager Tom Lasorda bleeds Dodger blue as he claims, then the color of Earl's blood is Oriole orange.

7

The Odd Couple

The clubhouse reeked of champagne and had the disheveled early-morning look of a place after an all-night party. It was but 12 hours ago that the Orioles had clinched the 1979 American League division title. Everything from Ken Singleton in tears to Don Stanhouse pouring champagne into the mouth of his stuffed gorilla made up the Saturday night scene. The Orioles were champions. On Sunday morning, Jim Palmer and Earl Weaver went to war—again. This time, Palmer wanted to do Weaver's job and Weaver, battling a hangover, was even more crude and ornery than usual. The results were a first-class fireworks display between the Orioles manager and his star pitcher.

Right after the Birds won the American League Eastern Division title, Earl Weaver said he was "going to get good and drunk." He suggested that the rest of his players do the same. Earl was true to his word and most of the Orioles followed his example.

Naturally, the Birds needed a massive dose of aspirin and sleep when they arrived at the park for a meaningless Sunday game with Cleveland. Jim Palmer was one of the few Orioles whose head was not pounding. Palmer doesn't drink. In fact, he refuses to consume any soft drink except diet soda because he had read that the large amounts of sugar in regular soda can cause tendonitis. So, the Palmer intellect remained sharp while the rest of the team's was cloudy.

As Weaver walked through the dressing room on this sleepy Sunday, he stopped by Palmer's locker.

"How's your elbow?" asked Weaver, recalling the latest of the various aches Palmer experienced during the year.

"My elbow will be good enough to start the fourth game of the playoffs," said Palmer.

Weaver stared at Palmer. For over a week, Earl had been saying Palmer would pitch the opening playoff game. Suddenly, the room exploded with screams from Weaver and Palmer. The rest of the team watched in wonder. They were at it again, the two who had been arguing for a dozen years.

"If I were managing the team," said Palmer, "I would not start Jim Palmer in the first playoff game. I would use Mike Flanagan. Flanagan is the best left-hander in baseball and the Cy Young Award winner. He should start the first game because then he could pitch in the fifth game if we need him. I could not go in the first and fifth games because of my arm."

Little coming from the mouth of Palmer stuns Weaver, but this did.

"If Jim is healthy enough to pitch the fourth game, why not the first?" asked Weaver, afterward. "I thought his arm was fine. I was shocked when he said he was hurting. I had been planning to use him in the first game for some time."

"Earl's logic is terrible," said Palmer. "It's not my job to manage, but his logic is still awful. I am sick of Earl because he's the manager and he thinks he is always right. That's a bunch of crap. The point is Flanagan is our best pitcher and he should go in the first and fifth games."

"I don't give a shit about the fifth game," said Weaver. "If Palmer wins the first game, there probably won't be a fifth game. If there is and Jim ain't healthy, I can use Steve Stone. Stone has not lost a game in two months. Jim is 4–1 with a 1.78 ERA in playoff competition. I want his experience in the opener."

Palmer then asked for a meeting with Weaver and Baltimore General Manager Hank Peters. "Earl gets irrational and unintelligible," he said. "I want to talk to Hank to get someone calm and lucid involved."

This session did not satisfy Palmer.

"They gave me an ultimatum," said Palmer. "Pitch the opener or go on the disabled list. So what can I do?"

"I didn't give Jim any ultimatum," countered Weaver. "I said, pitch the first game. If he ain't healthy enough to pitch the opener, then he is hurt."

"It's the manager's decision who to pitch," said Hank Peters. "Earl wants Palmer and I back him all the way. There is some merit to Jim's thoughts, but Earl's the manager and he has won an awful lot of games. Jim was given an order to pitch like a player is ordered to bunt. It's not an ultimatum."

"Jim always needs an excuse," said Weaver. "That way, he has an alibi if he fails. The thing is, he seldom needs an excuse and I don't think he will in the playoffs."

The next day, an opinion story was carried by the *Baltimore Evening Sun* under the headline PALMER SHOULD SHUT UP AND LET WEAVER MANAGE ripped the right-hander for questioning Weaver's decision. "For ten days, Weaver has said Palmer would pitch the opener and Palmer said little," said the story. "Sunday, his teammates were basking in the glow of what their teamwork, sacrifices, and sweat have yielded. Palmer should have joined them instead of stealing the spotlight." Palmer went into a rage over the article, underlining in red ink portions which he found objectionable.

Palmer did start the opener. He allowed three runs in nine innings, and Baltimore emerged a 6–3 victor over California in the tenth. The Birds eliminated the Angels in four games; Palmer's concern over a fifth contest was unnecessary.

Weaver and Palmer.

They are as much a part of the Baltimore scene as crabs and the Preakness. They are the two men most responsible for the Orioles' success during the last two decades and their influence

reaches far beyond their individual deeds. Pitching and the system have made the Orioles. There is no Oriole pitching manual
on sale, but there should be. Certainly there is enough material to
fill several volumes. Most of it has come from Palmer, Weaver,
and George Bamberger.

"Truthfully, the reason there has always been a lot of strong
pitching in the Orioles system is due mostly to the scouts," said
Bamberger. "Baltimore scouts find pitchers. Cincinnati and
Pittsburgh scouts sign hitters. I don't know why one organization can't find a pitcher and another can't sign a hitter, but it
happens."

Bamberger spent 17 years in the minors. His major league
experience consists of 14 innings. He is a legend in Vancouver,
British Columbia, where he was voted into that city's sports Hall
of Fame after spending seven years on its Pacific Coast League
team. He won 213 games in the bushes, threw a no-hitter and set
a Pacific Coast League record by not walking a batter in 68⅔
innings.

"He also had the best spitter in the minors," said Weaver. "He
calls it the 'Staten Island Sinker,' since he's from New York. He
taught it to Mike Caldwell when he was managing the Brewers."

Ray Miller assumed Bamberger's job in 1978. Like Bamberger,
Miller began as a minor league instructor for the Orioles. Miller
never hurled in the majors. At the end of his career, he was a
spitball pitcher. Miller and Bamberger are Weaver's kind of
coaches. Their major league experience is virtually nonexistent.
They spent almost an intolerable amount of time in the minors.
The game is at the center of their intellectual lives. They are
smart and they can teach. Nothing was easy for them, so they
understand that players have limitations, and they know the
value of patience. Weaver subscribes to the mainstream baseball
axiom that few Hall of Famers make great coaches or managers,
although he makes a large exception for Frank Robinson. That is
why Robinson was the only great player to serve as a coach under
Weaver.

What has made the Birds' pitching impeccable sounds elementary.

"When you sign with the Orioles, it is like going to school," said
young Baltimore pitcher Dave Ford. "It begins in rookie ball. For
me, that was in Bluefield, West Virginia. The first thing they told

me was I didn't have to strike everybody out. The second thing was not to walk anyone. The third thing was learn to throw a changeup. Immediately, they started working with me on these three things."

Baltimore pitchers are like a fine, compact automobile. There are few frills, but everything is functional. A little goes a long way and they seldom break down. Despite all his aches and complaints, Palmer has encountered few serious injuries since he came under Weaver and Bamberger. He also had become the role model for all Baltimore pitchers while Weaver, Bamberger, and Miller were and are the muses.

The brainwashing job goes something like this:

You may not have Palmer's talent or grace, but you can learn his control, his off-speed pitches and his training techniques. You too can win 20 games and the Cy Young Award. Palmer, Weaver, and the pitching coach [first Bamberger and now Ray Miller] will show you the way.

"The Orioles have a pitching institute," said Scott McGregor. "Here, it is no big deal to win 20 games. When you come to the Orioles, they make you a part of the system. They break you in as a long relief pitcher so you can pick up experience in situations that are not crucial. If you do well there, you become a starter. Every young pitcher on our staff went through this type of orientation. Even Jim Palmer was in the bullpen during his first year."

Of course, the Oriole scouts and men like former Minor League Director Jim McLaughlin lay the foundation for the pitching staff.

"The Orioles pay attention to two things when they sign players," said Bamberger. "First is talent. Next is attitude. They are far more aware of a player's attitude than most organizations. I know it sounds funny, but they are a happy family. They don't tolerate a pain in the neck because misery loves company. If they have a bad actor, they get rid of him. A bad kid will spoil a good one. Seldom does a good kid save a rotten one."

As Bamberger says, the Orioles could always find pitchers. In the early 1960s, the Birds produced Wally Bunker, Chuck Estrada, Jack Fisher, Tom Phoebus, and Jim Palmer. All had great arms. All developed arm problems under Pitching Coach Harry Brecheen.

Palmer says Brecheen seldom had the Orioles throw lightly.

When they did throw between starts, it was at a high exertion level. Bamberger and Miller feel the arm is like any other muscle. It needs to be stretched and exercised. If you were going to run a marathon every four days, you would not cover 26 miles and then sleep for three days before trying it again. It would be unfair to place all the blame for the pitchers' physical troubles on Brecheen, but they diminished once he and Hank Bauer were replaced by Weaver and Bamberger in 1968.

"I think the key thing is the way pitching methods are passed down from the Orioles to the minors," said Miller. "Everybody does it the same way. I signed with Cleveland and all they ever did was tell you to throw hard. They didn't have good coaches. No one taught you a changeup. If you don't learn it in the minors, you probably won't learn it in the majors. I remember when Early Wynn was coaching in the minors for Cleveland. He was famous for hitting batters, but he said we shouldn't do that. 'You're pissed at someone, wait until they get to first base and then drill them in the back while trying to pick them off.' Here is a guy who won 300 games in the majors and that was his main advice.

"I had two Minor League managers who were not exactly great teachers. One was Red Davis. A nice man, Red always said, 'Well fellows, let's just do what's right and keep our jobs.' That was it. The other manager was Phil Cavarretta. He would come out to the mound when you were in a tough spot and say, 'Come on, gutless, get the guy out.' Another great piece of advice."

With the Orioles, pitchers receive a lot of hints. Palmer has said Weaver often overdoes it. But it is hard to argue with the Birds' record. Time and time again, a veteran hurler comes to Baltimore and has the best season of his career. It has happened to Mike Cuellar, Steve Stone, Mike Torrez, Pat Dobson, and Rudy May.

"That is no accident," said Miller. "For example, Stone and Dobson joined us with four or five pitches which they threw from two or three different windups. Earl would ask them why they needed all those pitches and windups. Didn't they have a couple of things that worked well? He wants pitchers to simplify things. Our way is elementary, throw strikes, go with your best pitches. Don't fool around, let the defense work behind you."

While the Orioles' pitching makes them frightful to an opposing club, no one hurler is asked to carry the team. Weaver has a
complete staff in the truest sense of the word. Also, the Birds have
been a home run-hitting club during much of Weaver's reign.
The excellent pitching has dwarfed this fact, but Weaver will tell
you Dr. Long Ball is about on equal terms with the pitching in the
Orioles' operation. "Pitching and three-run homers, that's what
wins games," he says.

Here is how a new pitcher is indoctrinated into the Baltimore
system.

When Torrez joined the Orioles, Brooks Robinson took him
aside and told him to make the batters hit ground balls. At the
time, the Birds' infield was composed of four Gold Glove winners
with Robinson, Mark Belanger, Bobby Grich and Boog Powell.
While with Montreal, Torrez was convinced that strikeouts were
a panacea. Brooks said strikeouts were overrated. Torrez listened
and won 20 games for the first and only time of his career.

The transformation was even more evident with Steve Stone.
In 1979, Baltimore made the righthander its first major acquisi-
tion from the free agent market. They gave him a four-year,
$720,000 contract. That seems like cab fair compared with the
current baseball wage scale, but at the time, Stone's $180,000
annual salary placed him near the top of the Orioles' payroll. It
was only $60,000 less than Palmer's, who made an issue of it with
the front office on several occasions. To the Oriole players, Stone
seemed like an expensive luxury. General Manager Hank Peters
seemed to have taken leave of his senses, putting out big bucks for
a pitcher with a 67–72 lifetime record and a history of arm
trouble.

Like Dobson, Cuellar, Torrez, and May, Stone had been just
an ordinary pitcher with other organizatons. Writers laughed
when they learned Stone (who had never won more than 15
games in a season) had a $10,000 bonus clause in his contract if he
copped the Cy Young Award. In his first two years with Baltimore, Stone went 36–14, winning 25 games and the Cy Young
Award in 1980. After 1980, Stone was the one who did the
laughing. But there were plenty of shouting matches and heart-
aches during Stone's maiden season with the Orioles.

In his first seven starts, he was shelled for 10 home runs. He yielded 2.43 homers per nine innings. He used to say he was right on Roger Maris' pace of 61 in a season. He wondered if he should visit Lourdes. Weaver found none of it amusing. He bellowed at Stone for walking hitters. Earl believes the dreaded base on balls is the root of most evil for pitchers. Often, Stone would trudge into Weaver's office. The entire locker room could hear Earl's raspy voice bearing down on Stone with a wrath that is genuinely frightening. For his part, Stone is a gentle man. He was confused by Earl's conduct.

"No one ever yelled at me like he did," said Stone.

Yet, Weaver kept Stone in the starting rotation. He sent him to the mound with the credo Earl feels is crucial to successful pitching: "The object of the game is to make the batter hit the ball off stride or to throw a pitch for a strike that the batter isn't looking for."

Earl showed Stone detailed charts that outlined the tendencies of every opposing hitter. Every team keeps this sort of record, but the Orioles do it in far more depth and give them greater attention.

"I recognize what needs to be thrown to win games," said Weaver. "We give the pitchers extra information. I don't know if they know it or use it, but it helps some guys. Stone may not think so, but something helped him when he came here."

Stone says Weaver taught him how to win. By the end of 1979, he was 11–9. He did not lose a game after July 9. He had made it through his first year of the Baltimore pitching school. In 1980, he was ready for the honor courses with which he absorbed the Orioles' data, giving himself the edge to become the sixth Baltimore pitcher to win the Cy Young Award during Weaver's tenure. Stone deserves most of the credit. He made the adjustments. He learned to handle the pressure of pitching for Earl Weaver. In the middle of his career, he was willing to change his entire approach to the game.

"Stone is a classic example of what happens to a lot of pitchers who come to Baltimore," said Ray Miller. "They become a part of our system. They find out that the information we have can be useful to them. Earl believes in his cards which show how every batter should be pitched. Pitchers can disagree and say they get a hitter out a different way. Earl doesn't care as long as it works. But if it doesn't, there is hell to pay for going against Earl's charts."

In 1979, Sammy Stewart found that out the hard way. A rookie at the time, Stewart was pitching in the 15th inning of a game with the Royals. The Birds' book says never throw George Brett a fastball in the strike zone. Stewart was aware of that, but he thought he could trick Brett. He uncorked a fastball and Brett launched it more than 400 feet into the waterfalls over the Kansas City right field wall. Weaver started raving at Stewart from the moment the ball left Brett's bat. He screamed at Stewart as he walked off the field. He screamed at him in the dugout. He screamed at him in the runway leading into the clubhouse. Over and over again, he asked Stewart, "How could you be so fucking dumb? How the fuck could you throw a fucking fastball?" Stewart said nothing. He was near tears. But the point was made. Stewart would never deliver a fat fastball to Brett again. Nor would he try to outsmart the Birds' book.

Some like to say Weaver is the reason the Orioles have three Cy Young Award winners—Stone, Palmer, and Mike Flanagan—on the staff. Earl often comments that he has managed 20 of the 21 pitchers to win 20 games a season for the Orioles. "I missed only with Steve Barber, in 1963," says Weaver. "And I had Barber in the minors," Obviously, that is hyperbole as any member of the Orioles is quick to mention.

Palmer will tell you that Weaver's words of wisdom on the mound hardly sound like they had emanated from the mouth of Solomon. And Weaver will explain that Palmer doesn't listen. And Palmer will counter that Weaver never threw a curve in his life, so what does he know? And Weaver will reply that you don't have to throw a curveball to know what a good one looks like—after all, how many art critics can paint like Picasso? Palmer says Earl can be crude. Weaver says Palmer thinks too much and sometimes overreacts to a simple suggestion, treating it like an indictment of his very existence.

To comprehend the relationship between the pitcher and the manager is to understand what makes the Orioles click. The combination of Weaver and Palmer have been the team's Pacemaker.

Those who are close to Palmer describe him as sensitive and occasionally insecure. They take the position that Palmer's personality was totally shaped by his background.

Palmer was the adopted son of Moe and Polly Wiesen. He was

called Jim Wiesen for much of his early life. His father was a dress manufacturer and his mother ran a dress shop. Moe Wiesen was Jewish and Polly was Catholic. They lived at 1095 Park Avenue, along with a butler and a maid and spent summers at various resorts. The family also had a house in Westchester County. Jim had no idea his father was a sick man. Moe Wiesen had a heart condition for years. One morning when Jim was nine he went downstairs and found the house full of people. His father had died during the night.

After the father's death, Polly Wiesen moved the family (which also included Jim's adopted sister) to Whittier, California. Later, they resided in Beverly Hills. Under the sun and smog of Los Angeles, Polly met and later married a former film character actor, Max Palmer. Max made most of his fortune by running taverns at Santa Anita and Hollywood Park race tracks. The Palmers bought a mansion in Coldwater Canyon. Their neighbors were Tony Curtis and Janet Leigh. They lived on the lower acreage of what once was the James Cagney estate. In 1960, the Palmer family moved to Scottsdale, Arizona. A year before that, Jim had taken the last name of his stepfather. Jim is a legend in Arizona high school athletics. In his senior year, he was All-State in football (he caught 54 passes as a wide receiver), baseball, and basketball (he averaged 25 points and turned down a scholarship offer from UCLA where he would have played with Kareem Abdul-Jabbar). In addition to dazzling everyone with his pitching, he batted .483.

"Palmer was an awesome high school player," said Indians Manager Dave Garcia. "I was scouting for the Giants at the time and I remember watching him play center field. He could cover a lot of ground. He could throw. He could hit. On the baseball field there was nothing he couldn't do."

The Orioles offered Palmer a $50,000 bonus to sign with them in 1964. Jim took the contract and immediately added another responsibility—he married his high school sweetheart, Susan Ryan. Susie and Jim Palmer were considered the ideal baseball couple for more than a decade. But the two eventually grew apart and separated in the summer of 1981.

One year after turning pro Palmer was in the majors. He was 19, had pitched one season in Class A and left little doubt he was a major leaguer when he joined the Orioles in 1965. He was 5–4 out of the bullpen, but went 15–10 in the Birds' pennant-winning season of 1966. He also tossed a four-hit shutout against the Dodgers in the World Series. At 20 he seemed to have it all—talent, impeccable looks, a pretty wife, and an enviable future. Again, the word most often attached to Palmer's name was "destined." He was destined for greatness. He was destined for the Hall of Fame. He was destiny's child.

But Palmer and his fans could never guess what destiny had in store for him in 1967. It was the pitcher's obituary, the bum arm.

In 1966, Palmer worked 208 innings, far more than he had ever pitched before. That is an overload for any precocious, developing talent. When the season ended, he personally painted his house. But his right arm would have none of it. It began aching and didn't let up when Jim went to spring training in 1967. He started the season with Baltimore but soon was sent to Rochester. When Class AAA failed to heal his elbow problem, the Orioles hoped the sun would. They shipped him to Class A Miami. None of it worked. At this point, Jim had altered his windup to compensate for his arm injury. In the process he developed a bad back. In 1967–68, he bounced from Elmira to Rochester to Miami. Most of the time he was unable to pitch.

But Palmer did take the mound a few times in Rochester. His manager was Earl Weaver, and it is here the great Palmer–Weaver debates were born. Jim loves to tell the story of a game between Rochester and Buffalo in 1967. Palmer was struggling throughout, often behind in the count. Then he walked the bases full. Weaver was steaming.

"Ah, throw this hamburger a strike," Earl yelled to Palmer. "This guy won't hit it. Throw it down the middle."

So Palmer tossed the batter a half-assed fastball, and the "hamburger" hit it half way to Canada. The guy Weaver thought was nothing more than a *Big Mac* was future Hall of Famer Johnny Bench.

By 1969 Palmer had regained his health. He likes to say he did it on his own, with little help from the Orioles. Their answer for an ulnar nerve ailment was Florida sunshine, but Palmer says that was simplistic. They also hinted that his arm did not really hurt . . . at least not as much as Palmer claimed it did. Jim still resents this charge, and it is the basis of his constant preoccupation with his health.

In the Oriole clubhouse, Palmer's ailments are treated lightly.

"Jim won 20 games for the eighth time in 1978 and then someone gave him a copy of 'Gray's Anatomy' and he hasn't been the same since," said Mike Flanagan with a smile. "It's tough to adjust to a new injury every start."

"I hate to see a story in the newspaper about some new type of injury," said Weaver. "Sure enough, Jim will come up with it. The guy doesn't know what it means to be human. He never gets a toothache. He always feels perfect. When some everyday sort of ache comes up, he thinks it's a big deal because it's new to him. I really think Jim should go to a hypnotist. It helped Paul Blair. It might make Jim feel better, help him finish games."

Weaver is fascinated by hypnotism. He has read books on the subject and has been known to put people in a trance while sitting at a dinner table. He does it by waving a spoon back and forth in front of their eyes. Of course, Earl knows Jim would not be an ideal subject. The two probably would argue about whether a teaspoon or a tablespoon were the proper instrument.

To his credit, Palmer does everything within his power to retain his impeccable physical condition. He is always rested and is a superb example of what happens when a pitcher does extra running and exercises. He does not carry excess body fat, which is why he became a model for Jockey shorts. With all that in mind, it is difficult to comprehend his preoccupation with physical problems.

The 1979 season was a typical example of Jim Palmer turning a year into one long episode of "General Hospital." He arrived in Miami on February 22 for spring training. As always, he was in enviable physical condition. His teammates are well aware that Jim falls prey to more ailments than Job, but even they were surprised when he made one lob in a game of catch and immediately retired to the trainer's room with a pain in the lower lumbar region of his back.

After much consultation the back problem was blamed on the long drive from Baltimore to Miami as Palmer pushed his Mercedes (complete with ACE license plates) at a 75 mph clip. Then again, it could have been something stemming from too much winter racquetball. Or maybe it was the change of climate.

"Who knows?" asked Weaver. "In 1978, he said he had shoulder troubles and missed the first two starts of the season. Then he threw a two-hit shutout at Milwaukee. He'll be ready."

Weaver was unconcerned. In fact, he gave the anxious press some material they could pass on to Palmer.

"The Chinese tell time by the Year of the Dragon and the Year of the Horse," said Weaver. "I tell time by Palmer. There was the Year of the Shoulder. The Year of the Ulnar Nerve. The Year of the Elbow. I guess this will be the Year of the Back."

When the writers relayed Weaver's needling to Palmer, Jim was placid.

"Hey, this is no big deal in the scheme of life," said Palmer. "But I don't know if I'll be ready to pitch the opener."

Palmer and Weaver spend most spring trainings debating this question: Will Jim be well enough to pitch opening day? Palmer says no. Weaver says yes. Then, Palmer says maybe. Weaver says absolutely. Until 1979, Jim would bitch and then go out and pitch. He used the threat of injury to taunt Earl, to keep the press occupied and to break the boredom of spring training.

But all that was to change in 1979. He would win only 10 games and spend more time in doctors' offices than on the mound.

There was much speculation that Palmer was actually using his pains to gain a new contract. In fact, he often joked that most of the pain was coming from his "renegotiation muscle." Jim then would shift into his usual contract tirade. He was earning $260,000 a season on a contract that ran through 1981.

"There are 20 pitchers in baseball making more money than I," Palmer frequently said. "Do you think there are 20 pitchers who are better than I was in the 1970s?"

If he was especially enthralled by his own rhetoric at the moment, Palmer would name some of those 20 hurlers and their salaries.

"I have to look out for my interests," added Palmer. "You can't be sure what this organization will do. Brooks Robinson asked them to take care of him and they told him to take a hike. The front office can be juvenile. I get a bonus [$30,000] if I start 30 games. I get credit for it even if I'm hurt and can't get through the first inning. All I have to do is start. That kind of thing shows you how far behind the times the Orioles are. They think they can motivate players with incentives. It's a joke."

Throughout the 1970s, Palmer complained about the Birds' reluctance to sign free agents or keep their own players from jumping to other clubs.

In 1976, Palmer assessed the Orioles' front office this way: "It is like going to a Cadillac dealer and saying, 'I'd really like to buy your car, but I'm only going to give you $10,000, not $14,000 because that is all I think it is worth.' If you do that, you just get laughed at, and the players are laughing at the Orioles' offers. If the Orioles are going to commit themselves to mediocrity, then maybe they better trade a Jim Palmer or Mark Belanger now while they have top value. They can get a couple of young and not too expensive players for each of us and build for the future. I've talked to other players. I know what they are getting. It's frightening. Cleveland gave Wayne Garland $2 million and he won 20 games only once. Reggie Jackson will get $3 million and he is an average player. He is not even a real good player. He doesn't throw, field or run the bases that well. He doesn't even hit that well, except for home runs."

When Jackson joined the Orioles in 1976, Palmer appeared to be jealous. While Jackson was holding out, demanding that the Birds renegotiate his contract, Palmer said he "lost respect for Jackson." At the time Palmer was earning $175,000 and Jackson was demanding $600,000.

"Is the Messiah coming back or what?" asked Palmer. "We have started playing and he has hurt the club by not showing up. Do you think it ever occurred to Jackson that there are 24 other guys counting on him?"

In defense of Palmer, most of his teammates felt the same way about Reggie Jackson.

"When Reggie finally did sign and play, we all knew he would be a free agent at the end of the year," said Ken Singleton. "The last road trip was something else. He would go into every city and size it up. In Cleveland he said he would never play there because there weren't enough writers."

Even though they often concurred with him, most of the Birds were weary of hearing Palmer's complaints.

"Jim was underpaid in the 1970s," said Singleton. "But so were most of us."

At times, former Oriole Lee May would silence Palmer during one of his contract laments.

"Hey, Jim," May would yell across the clubhouse. "Who held the gun to your head?"

"What gun?" asked Palmer.

"The gun they put to your head when they made you sign your contract."

"You know what Jim would like?" asked one player. "To be on the second year of a four-year contract and to be renegotiating a new four-year pact at the same time."

If Palmer wanted a reason for his contract dilemma, he only had to look in the mirror. Jim served as his own agent. While witty and intelligent, he was no match for the Oriole front office at the bargaining table.

The persistent haggling over dollars did not end until the middle of 1980, when Palmer hired Ed Keating as an agent and received a contract calling for $600,000 a summer. Before 1980 many had said Palmer purposely settled for a relatively low price as a defense mechanism. He would rebel when reading or hearing how great he should be. Some coaches and writers claimed he should be a 30-game winner and anything less was his fault. By taking less money, he could rationalize away a substandard performance. Like his health, it is another of his defense mechanisms—his alibis, as Weaver calls them.

Naturally, Jim could then rant and rave about his salary. It is interesting since he was raised in wealth and never lacked for anything materialistic. But some say Palmer always expected to earn millions because he came from a rich family.

Palmer spends so much of his career attacking the front office, Weaver, his teammates or whatever else catches his fancy, that some Baltimore fans have lost sight of his achievements. He is the first American League pitcher since Lefty Grove to win 20 games eight times. He also holds the majors' best winning percentage and the second lowest earned run average.

Additionally, he has served as the national chairman for the Cystic Fibrosis Foundation and frequently visits the patients in various hospitals. For the most part, he sets an excellent example for younger Oriole pitchers.

"He is like having another pitching coach around," said Ray

Miller. "When the other pitchers see a guy like Palmer working hard and taking care of himself, it does more good than anything you can tell them."

"Palmer is a great pitcher, certainly one of the all-time greats," says Weaver. "I can't count all the big games he has won for us. Even when he was hurt in 1979, he snapped our longest losing streak of the year by beating the Yankees. He won our first game in two years in Kansas City. He has risen to the occasion as much as any pitcher in baseball. He is a great pitcher even when he is a little tired or not 100%. That is something Jim does not believe, however."

A number of players asked, "Did Jim say forearm or forehead," when Palmer revealed one of his arm ailments. And Palmer has said, "I think I'll go to Dr. Kerlan [the famed orthopedist] for a brain scan."

Part of the reason the spats between Weaver and Palmer loom larger than they should is that both men have elephant-like memories. Palmer can give a pitch-by-pitch account of some of his minor league games in the middle 1960s. When players argue over some event from the Orioles' past, Palmer often acts as the judge, delivering what all know will be the proper sequence and facts of games or seasons most have long forgotten.

But even Palmer cannot recall every verbal joust he has had with Earl. Here are some of the most infamous.

●During a 1969 game with the Senators Palmer took a 7–1 lead into the ninth inning. Then Washington roughed him up for four more runs, giving him a 7–5 victory. That raised Palmer's record to 10–3, but he was acting like the "unhappiest 10–3 pitcher in baseball history," according to the *Baltimore Evening Sun* baseball writer Phil Jackman. Palmer was in a rage. It was as though he had been driven from the game in the second inning after being pounded for 10 runs.

"I haven't the slightest idea what Palmer is mad at," said Weaver. "I know it is me. But he won't tell me."

Meanwhile, Palmer was saying he might not make his next start because of a blister on his throwing hand which would prohibit him from using his curveball. This ruffled Weaver.

"If he can't pitch, hell, somebody else will," cried Weaver. "If he's got a blister, let him go on the disabled list . . . I don't know, maybe he feels he should have come out of the game earlier. Maybe he's right, but he had an easy eighth inning. I thought I'd give him a chance to complete the game."

Palmer was far more concerned with his earned run average. He felt Weaver should have yanked him earlier and spared him the four runs he yielded in the ninth. This would be the script for most of the Weaver–Palmer feuds. Earl wanting Jim to stay in a game, Palmer asking out.

• Palmer still calls Arlington Stadium the "Eye of the Hurricane." It all began in a 1978 game in Texas when Jim threw the Rangers' Juan Beniquez a fastball that he rapped for a double. These days Palmer calls the hit "windblown." Weaver says Palmer made a stupid pitch, giving a notorious fastball hitter like Beniquez something he could handle. That is what Weaver told Palmer when he walked to the mound following Beniquez' smash. Then came the debate. Weaver has his record cards, which he feels dictate the way hitters should be pitched. Palmer has his memory, which is almost infallible. Both men have experienced success in their own way, and the last thing they want to hear is a second-guess from anyone.

The screaming began.

Weaver said Palmer should have used his slider. Palmer asked Earl where he had been for the last few years.

"I don't even throw a slider," Palmer said.

"You have a great slider," said Weaver. "Use it."

"It hurts my arm," said Palmer. "Besides, it was not a good pitch in that situation to Beniquez. He can't hit a low-outside fastball."

Palmer says he would have tolerated Earl's tirade if the team had been winning. But he was sick of it. Sick of what he thought was Earl's obvious stupidity on this subject. And sick of Earl's second-guessing only when the Birds were behind in the score. Sick of Earl saying "we" when the team was going well and "they" when it was in a slump.

"Here, you can pitch if you think you can do better," said Palmer, handing Earl his glove.

That shifted everything into high gear. They screamed at each other on the mound. When Jim was removed from the game, they screamed at each other in the dugout. Palmer says Weaver was jumping up and down, "acting like a maniac." Earl says Palmer showed him up. Palmer says that Earl swore at him and that he would embarrass him at every opportunity. Later, they screamed at each other in the clubhouse.

The Orioles lost the game and Weaver wanted to discuss what happened on the mound with Palmer. Jim refused.

"So you quit," asked Weaver.

"No, I'll pitch somewhere else," said Palmer. He refused to meet with Earl in the manager's office, so Weaver had the doors closed to keep the media out and addressed the entire team.

"Who wants to be traded?" yelled Weaver.

No hands were raised.

"That guy over there does," Weaver said pointing at Palmer.

"That's really bush, Earl," Palmer grumbled and was then chased into the trainer's room by Weaver.

Palmer claims that Weaver apologized to him the next day.

●In another game in 1978, following that storm in Texas, Palmer had a five-hit shutout over the White Sox in the sixth inning. He motioned to the dugout for Weaver to come out. Earl did not appear. An inning later, Palmer gave up a pair of hits. This time, Earl did come to the mound and replaced him with Don Stanhouse. Stanhouse preserved the shutout. All should have been well. At least, that is what you would expect. But, you seldom get what you are looking for from Palmer and Weaver. After the game, Palmer explained that he had a sore neck.

"I was as surprised as anybody in the world that Jim had a neck problem," said Weaver. "It is Jim's fault for not telling me. I'd have gone out there when he looked to the dugout, but I didn't see him. I don't watch him 100% of the time. I'm sorry if it took a few extra seconds."

"I don't like to talk to Weaver," replied Palmer, when asked by the press why he did not inform Weaver of his troubles. "Earl annoys me."

Sensing another Weaver–Palmer fight in the making, the writers relayed Palmer's words to Earl.

"I annoy him!" cried Weaver. "That's tough. We didn't have a spat. I don't know why he said that. It sure will look good in print though, won't it."

Later, Palmer and Weaver spoke about the tiff.

"Do you think I was serious when I said that stuff?" asked Palmer.

"The writers thought you were," said Weaver, storming away.

All of this happened after the first game of a doubleheader. During the second game, Palmer called the press box to clarify his statement.

"What I meant was, I thought he ignored me when I asked to come out," said Palmer. "I must annoy him."

•One incident in Minnesota on June 17, 1979 will be forever known as the "Father's Day Affair."

"See this head of gray hair?" asked Earl Weaver taking his hat off. "Every one of them belongs to Jim Palmer. Frank Robinson and Brooks Robinson never gave me a gray hair. Neither did Al Bumbry. Palmer has me aggravated. I really don't care if he ever pitches for this club. It's the same thing, day after day, city after city."

This verbal volley between the Orioles' pair stemmed from an article in the *St. Paul Pioneer Press.* It came in a Palmer interview in which the star pitcher restated many of his old complaints. He wanted to leave Baltimore. He was underpaid. It bothered him to pitch against someone like Dennis Eckersley who was making $300,000 more than Palmer. When this occurs, Palmer says, "I don't feel as motivated as I should be." He concluded the interview by saying that he was going "to aggravate them until they trade me."

All of this was with the same timing as Jimmy Carter's "Ethnic Purity" remarks. The Birds were in first place, having pulled together to try to win a pennant and perhaps even save the franchise from moving to Washington. With Palmer not pitching because of arm problems, many were now starting to wonder if his ailments were merely a façade. There was speculation that he was engaged in a power play to force the O's to give him more money or deal him to a team that would. Palmer had missed five starts, including his last three. When Jim said he was hurting, he was rested. When he wanted to go to Los Angeles to be examined by Dr. Robert Kerlan, the ballclub sent him to the West Coast. In other words, the Birds gave him everything short of a new contract. Palmer also said that he would like to help broadcast the World Series. "I'd be watching it anyway, so why not?"

"Jim can broadcast the second, third, fifth and sixth games," said Weaver. "But he'll be pitching in the first, fourth and seventh games."

"Look, we're out to win—with or without Palmer," said Ken Singleton. "We need Jim because he's a great player. The guys here want to win this thing badly. Maybe getting the measley $30,000 World Series share doesn't mean much to him, but it does to the other 24 players. Besides, the big thing is the prestige that comes with winning."

A copy of the Palmer article was left by Weaver in Jim's locker. Written across it was: "HAPPY FATHER'S DAY—NOW GROW UP."

"It's time for Jim to act his age," said Weaver. "He's 33 years old. Look, the man has done a lot for me. I'd like him to get his money, but he signed a contract so there's nothing I can do. The whole thing isn't my fault or Hank Peters' or Jerry Hoffberger's [former owner of the Orioles]. It's Palmer's. He'll pitch Tuesday and we'll see if he's worth the $260,000. Palmer can tighten his belt, play out his option and try his luck on the open market when his contract is up. He's the only one who can do it. That's the same thing I told my son when he was 22."

"Palmer wondered what everyone was so excited about.

"There's nothing new," said Jim. "I've said all these things before. I want to leave, but it's a matter of money. I have nothing against the players or anyone else. I'd think Earl would have more to worry about than this. As for Earl's gray hair, I think he got a lot of them from watching [former O's catcher] Earl Williams."

"If Palmer was smart he would shut up," said Coach Frank Robinson. "He isn't as smart as he thinks he is."

"The players are sympathetic to Jim," said Rick Dempsey. "He deserves more money and maybe the ballclub should eat a little crow, swallow some pride and pay him what he's worth. We need Jim to win a pennant because he's been there before.

"I don't like a lot of things he says, but he has helped the pitching staff by working with guys like Dennis Martinez and others. Maybe if they gave him more money he'd change. The only thing that bothers some players is that he isn't pitching. The guy could pitch with a little pain and still win with just his fastball. The feeling toward him would probably be a lot worse if we were losing."

Palmer did pitch that Tuesday and was a 4–1 winner over Cleveland.

Other than the pitchers, few Orioles like Jim. Most respect him. All wish he had more patience. Palmer has the habit of tossing his fielders a dark, cold stare if they commit an error behind him. His face will take on an expression of complete shock when he yields a broken-bat hit. How dare he be so unlucky? He believes he can be perfect on almost every pitch, and he expects his fielders to do the same on every ball hit in their direction. When they aren't he has been known to embarrass them by raising his hands in disgust.

Two players that Palmer has had small battles with are Doug DeCinces and former Oriole Pat Kelly.

The first took place in a 1978 game. It was the eighth inning, Baltimore had a 1–0 lead, and Palmer seemed on the verge of his 20th victory. Cleveland's Jim Norris hit a foul ball down the left field line. Kelly dashed for the ball. After a long sprint, he saw it bounce in and then out of his glove, landing on the ground. One pitch later, Palmer took himself out of the game, complaining of elbow pains. Don Stanhouse replaced Palmer, and the Indians went on to win, 2–1.

That was the third time in 1978 had Palmer made a quick exit because of alleged ailments. His teammates had their doubts. Mark Belanger and Ken Singleton both suggested, "Palmer doesn't want to work under pressure."

"When Palmer left the game," said Belanger, "in effect, he said 'Don't we have an outfielder here who can catch the ball?' I thought Pat Kelly made a helluva effort. I don't want any pitcher on this club to get on any fielder, and that's what Jim has been doing. I'm tired of it. The impression is that we're not trying for the man, and that isn't fair. These guys bust their butts for him. In fact, they may even try harder because he's a great pitcher. If he is hurt, it's an entirely different story. I guess some people can endure pain and some can't. But this isn't the first time. The last three or four times, he begged out when it got tough."

"It seems to me he doesn't want to pitch under pressure sometimes," said Singleton. "I don't blame him. It's not easy. But every game can't be 6–2 or 5–1. Sometimes you have to win, 1–0."

Interestingly, Kelly refused to rap Palmer. A devout Christian,

Kelly believes it is best to turn the other cheek. With Palmer, he had plenty of practice. It seemed Kelly's fielding miscues always occurred whenever Palmer was on the mound. In 1978, Kelly had the misfortune of having not one, but two balls pop out of his glove and over the fence behind him. They were ruled home runs. Palmer was pitching both times. In the spring of 1979, one of Palmer's favorite lines was, "This year, Earl is teaching Kelly to knock the ball back in play and hold everything to a double."

Weaver's reaction to the Kelly–Palmer problem also was intriguing.

"Nobody in baseball has the right to point a finger at anyone else," said Weaver. "But you can understand why it happened when a player whose arm was bothering him wants to win. If Palmer did say those things about Kelly, I am sure he is sorry."

General Manager Hank Peters tried to quiet the controversy, saying, "It was unfortunate, but since it occurred we will have to live with it. It's another page in the history of the Orioles. I think everybody has a breaking point past which they cannot go without making some sort of comment."

Another time when Weaver and Peters made life easier for Palmer was in June of 1981. This time Palmer pulled himself out of a game after two innings. Ostensibly, it was because of a sore neck, but he hinted that Doug DeCinces' play at third base did little to comfort him.

That sent DeCinces into a rage.

"What gives Palmer the right to continually downgrade everyone who plays behind him?" asked DeCinces. "Jim seems to forget that the same players win games for him. I don't think it is fair that he shows up guys on the field and says he gets no support. Everybody makes physical errors, but we don't throw our hands up in the air when someone hits a home run off Jim. I don't think it is right that he says things behind people's backs. This is a 24-man team and one prima donna."

In recent years DeCinces' views have reflected those held by many of the Orioles. Few have been willing to state it so bluntly, however. By the same token, DeCinces does not like to put his body in front of hot smashes down the third base line. He has had his nose broken four times because of bad hops, making him somewhat timid. This was at the center of Palmer's complaints.

Palmer and DeCinces have been at odds for some time.

"Doug took a cheap shot at me in 1977 and I had the opportunity to reciprocate, but I considered it unfair," said Palmer. "Why should I talk to Doug about these things? It wouldn't do any good. If I seemed to offend him by being upset that the ball wasn't caught, it is just a matter of fact. If that play isn't made, you don't win unless you get six or seven runs. Doug knows how he played that ball. I can't play third for him. I know he is worried about his nose. But that doesn't help me. It was nothing personal, just a matter of winning or losing."

"Jim is an emotional person," said Weaver. "A lot of times on the mound he gets disgusted with himself, or with the way things are going. But, in front of 50,000 people, it looks like you're arguing. I see no cause for concern. The third baseman wants the pitcher to do a little better and the pitcher wants the third baseman to do a little better. So I hope we all do a little better and kiss and make up. Some guys get angry and do better. The judge gave me custody of both of them [Palmer and DeCinces], so I don't worry about things like this."

Weaver is well aware of what the team thinks of Palmer. For this reason he tries to defuse the criticism. Idiosyncrasies or not, Palmer is still a valuable member of the Orioles, and Weaver wants to keep peace in the clubhouse. If there is to be a war the manager wants to start it so that he can control it.

"Earl and Palmer are a lot alike," said Oriole Coach Elrod Hendricks. "They are high strung and they want to win so badly. They never leave anything unsaid. When they are in a bad mood, they seem to seek out each other. I think they use this kind of relationship to break the monotony. They almost always fight about Jim staying in games. Earl will tell Jim he is a Hall of Famer, and therefore he should finish the game. Jim will say he is tired or hurting."

"To me, all those problems between Earl and Palmer are nothing," said Orioles Scout Jim Russo. "It is one of those things where they each want to get in the last word. Whoever does thinks he has won. Earl loves to needle and so does Jim. The press hears them and thinks they are at each other's throats. Don't kid yourself. Earl knows how to handle Palmer. He likes to yell, especially at pitchers, and some resent it. He is always asking a pitcher why he threw a certain pitch in a certain spot if it is something he wasn't supposed to use."

"The big point of contention between Jim and Earl is finishing games," said George Bamberger. "From the seventh inning on, Jim was as great a pitcher as there ever was. He knew how to finish a game. Lately, he has changed. Maybe he has lost confidence in himself late in the game. I remember how Earl used to tell Palmer, 'You're the greatest pitcher in the game, finish it yourself.' Then Palmer would say something about his arm stiffening up. But you can't blame Earl. Who is better than Palmer? Earl's attitude is, 'here's the ball, now go out and pitch.'"

"Earl and Palmer are like father and son," said Ray Miller. "Palmer has about 20% of Earl's wins and he never lets him forget it. Their fights are bizarre, the conversations hard to follow. During the game, when Palmer isn't pitching, they talk to each other. Palmer is a thinking man. He will ask Earl about certain strategies and other things. Sometimes Palmer will second-guess him. Earl enjoys it. He often says Jim would make a good manager."

"Father and son," "the odd couple" and many other labels have been placed on Weaver and Palmer. The consensus is that they revel in their bickering, much like a man and woman with a 25-year marriage. It is a classic "I can't live with you and I can't live without you" relationship.

Weaver and Palmer are very similar. They are successful and know it. They have a wealth of energy. They even share the same hobby—gardening. Neither will admit it, but they are both perfectionists.

Palmer strongly denies this. He says people just think he is a perfectionist. He claims everyone, including Weaver, expects him to throw a complete game and win every time he takes the mound. He notes that while some pitchers are supposed to win 20 games, everyone expects 30-win seasons from him.

"Sometimes on the mound, I'll tell Earl my arm is stiff and he tells me I am a Cy Young Award winner," said Palmer. "What kind of dumb remark is that? He doesn't listen to me. If he would listen, it would be easier for all concerned."

Palmer is correct on this point. Earl is not a good listener. Of course, neither is Palmer.

"You know what the ultimate test is for a Timex watch?" Palmer likes to ask. "It is taping it to Earl's tongue. Really, he is too silly and juvenile to hate. Besides, Earl is not afraid to apologize. He is funny. When we are leaving runners on third base with less than two outs, Earl sometimes says something like he never left a runner on third when he played. I remember Dave McNally saying, 'Yeah, but you never got out of the Western League.' That really pissed Earl off. McNally handled Earl well. When Earl would say things to him he would just go 'Hmmm.' It comes down to this, instead of having my parents scream at me I have Earl Weaver."

The key is respect. Both men have it for the other.

"I'll say this for Jim, he is one of the few guys who always cheers in the dugout," said Earl. "Not too many guys do that anymore."

"Whatever Earl has done has been in my best interests," Palmer has admitted in mellower moments. "He demands the same thing of all his players."

Weaver enjoys taunting Jim by calling out the number of games Palmer has won during his career. Palmer is always within hearing range and he quickly realizes that Weaver's number is low and informs Earl that he is wrong. "But I only count the ones you won for me," says Weaver.

"Jim has won 20% of my games," said Weaver. "I have sent him to the mound over 300 times, and Jim will tell you he could have won 300 if I had done *my* job right. I'd love to see him win 300. He is in perfect condition. You know, Jim and I probably have not gone more than a month without talking. In his last year, Dave McNally wouldn't talk to me. Now, we're friends. Jim and I are friends, too. But we're not father and son. A father can spank his son. I can't do that to Palmer."

8

Baseballs' Son of Sam

Earl Weaver was standing in the corner of the Orioles dugout. The game had just begun and Baltimore pitcher Mike Flanagan had thrown two balls to the first batter.

"Where were those pitches?" Weaver shrieked at home plate umpire Bill Haller. "You go to bed last night? Did you get any sleep?"

Then Weaver slipped into the dugout runway and lit up a Raleigh. Another ball was called.

"Ray," Earl said to Orioles Pitching Coach Ray Miller, "we ain't gonna win if Flanagan don't throw no strikes. What's wrong, he like walking guys? Three-and-oh on the first batter. Doesn't he want to throw strikes?"

Then Weaver turned toward the field.

"Throw strikes," he yelled to Flanagan.

"Earl never shuts up in the dugout," says Ken Singleton. "He talks for nine innings. The only guys who go near him are Ray Miller and sometimes Palmer. Most of the time, the stuff he says is pretty funny."

More than any other manager, Earl turns the dugout into theatre. When not on his players, he is shouting at the umpires.

"Umpires have told me they can't concentrate with Earl

screaming at them all the time," said Elrod Hendricks. "When I used to catch for the Orioles, I would sometimes tell Earl the calls were not as bad as they looked if I thought Earl's getting on the umpires would only make things worse."

On this day, Weaver continued to hammer away. The first base umpire was Bill Haller, one of Earl's old adversaries. They have disagreed for over a decade. Neither is surprised by the actions of the other. But this game was an exception. Haller was wearing a microphone for a "PM Magazine" show in Washington. Earl didn't know it, and when Haller called a balk on Flanagan the tape gave everyone a chance to hear exactly what was said between Weaver and the umpire.

WEAVER: "That was no balk! No way! No way!"

HALLER: "Behind the rubber, behind it. It came off . . ."

W: "Ah, bullfeathers."

H: "Bullfeathers yourself."

W: " You're here and your crew is here to screw us. You're awful. You can't do nothing right."

H: "You run yourself, Earl, you run yourself . . . [Weaver has just been ejected] . . . You hit me?"

W: "Yeah, because you put your finger on me. Do it agian and I'll knock you on your ass."

H: "Yeah, sure."

W: "Yeah, you're here for a specific reason."

H: "Yeah, what's that?"

W: "To do a number on us . . . do that again [touch me] and I'll knock you right on your nose."

H: "Ah, Earl, you're not going to knock anybody on their ass."

W: "Ah, you're full of shit."

H: "I didn't touch you."

W: "You're lying."

H: "You're lying."

W: "No, you are."

H: "No, you are."

W: "No, you are."

W: "You're no good."

H: "You're no good."

W: "No, you ain't no good."

H: "You ain't neither."

W: "You're here to screw us and you'll have your chance tomorrow [when Haller was due to work behind the plate]. What are you doing here now?"

H: "Why don't you call the league office and ask 'em?"

W: "I will."

H: "Good."

W: "Don't think I won't?"

H: "Do it."

Weaver started to leave and then came back: "You ain't going nowhere."

Haller: "You aren't either."

Weaver: "Wait five or 10 years from now and let's see who's in the fucking Hall of Fame."

H: "Ha, you're going to be in the Hall of Fame?"

W: "You know it."

H: "For fucking up the World Series?"

W: "You know it."

H: "For fucking up the World Series?"

W: "I've won more than I've lost."

H: "No you haven't, Earl [meaning World Series games]."

W: "Games...games...I'm talking about [regular season] games."

H: "You better get going, Earl."

W: "You had your hands on me."

H: "Wrong, Earl, wrong."

There are several interesting aspects of this conversation. After the first two exchanges, the balk call was completely ignored. It then degenerated into a personal feud between Haller and Weaver, with dialogue fitted more to 10-year-olds than to two successful baseball men. There is a reason they are called the "Boys of Summer."

It was later discovered that Weaver may have been set up. Orioles General Manager Hank Peters complained to the American League hierarchy, saying Haller should not have been permitted to wear a microphone. Supervisor of Umpires Dick Butler also indicated that Haller had not received permission to be wired. For this reason many of the Orioles thought Haller had intentionally provoked Weaver with a poor call so that he could get one of Earl's tirades on tape for the public to hear. The umpires say that would be questioning their integrity, and that although they may not like Earl, they would never pull a cheap stunt of that sort. This is just an example of what it is like to be an umpire with Earl Weaver raging at you.

The Weaver—Haller tape became a collector's item among baseball writers. Most of them in Baltimore have a copy of it. It is baseball's version of the Watergate tapes. At the 1980 baseball winter meetings in Dallas, it was played several times in the press room to the delight of writers and baseball executives from across the country.

Earl Weaver's battles with the umpires and the baseball establishment are long and legendary. Each side has a list of transgressions against the other, although Weaver does not hold lengthy grudges against most umpires. Make no mistake, some umpires hate Earl Weaver. They have said it time and again. But most of them also respect him. With the possible exception of (former ump) Ron Luciano, Weaver does not hate any umpire. He simply feels it is a part of his job to be constantly badgering them, clawing for every call, every judgment and every rule interpretation to go his way. Earl is also well aware that attacking umpires only increases his popularity with the fans. As former Orioles Minor League Director Jim McLaughlin has said, Earl may tolerate flaws in ballplayers, but umpires must be perfect.

The same is true of league officials.

Umpires profess that Earl knows the rules better than any other manager. The subtleties and nuances found in the back pages of the rule book in fine print do not escape Weaver, even if he needs his glasses to read every word. He is always creating a crisis for American League President Lee MacPhail and Baseball Commissioner Bowie Kuhn.

For example, in the 1979 World Series Kuhn ordered players

not to wear wool ski caps while on the diamond or in the dugout. There was snow on the ground in Baltimore, and the windchill factor made it feel like 15 degrees that Fall. The players wanted the caps for warmth. They mentioned it to Weaver, who immediately pulled out his rulebook. He meticulously covered every page and the result was exactly as he had thought—there was no mention of ski caps. He relayed this information to Kuhn. The Commissioner was in a quandary and a meeting was called. A compromise was struck which permitted players to don ski caps in the bullpen, but not in the dugout or on the playing field.

On another occasion, September 15, 1977 in Toronto, Weaver pulled the Orioles off the field and forfeited a contest to the hapless Blue Jays in the middle of a pennant race. It was the fifth inning. Toronto had a 4–0 lead. Weaver was complaining about a tarpaulin placed over the Blue Jays' bullpen near the left field foul line. He felt that the tarp was a safety hazard to the players, and he expressed these sentiments to umpire Marty Springstead, who said he could not order the removal of the tarp. With the support of his players, Earl decided to take his team off the field and refuse to play unless the tarp was put elsewhere. The tarp remained, the Blue Jays were awarded a victory and the Birds dropped 2½ games behind the first place Yankees. Some criticized Weaver for his actions. How could he give away a game in the midst of a pennant drive?

"I would never put winning a game ahead of the safety of my players," said Weaver. "I would rather play the last 16 games with everyone healthy than risk having a career ruined because someone ran into the tarp. I knew my options at the time. I told the players I thought I was right and it was their decision to back me. They did. I had never seen a forfeit, but I had never seen anyone cover up part of the field, either."

Following the 1977 season, an edict from the American League office forbade the Blue Jays from keeping their tarp so close to the field.

Earlier in 1977 Weaver had scored a victory over the same umpire, Springstead. The Birds were playing in Cleveland and had lost the first game of a doubleheader, putting them in a precarious position in the nightcap.

It was the bottom of the ninth. Baltimore had a 3–2 lead with two outs. Cleveland had Duane Kuiper on third and Jim Norris at first. Paul Dade tapped a ground ball to Orioles second baseman Rich Dauer. Dauer bobbled it, picked it up and heaved it into the dugout. Kuiper and Norris both scored on the play and it looked as though the Tribe was a 4–3 winner. Both teams left the field. Cleveland radio station WWWE began to windup its broadcast with sportscaster Joe Tait saying, "The Indians win. The game is over. Final score, 4–3."

"Wasn't this a wonderful evening," added Herb Score, the Indians' other announcer. "That second victory made it so sweet."

In Baltimore, television and radio stations cut to commercials, explaining that the Orioles had lost both games.

Everyone was sure it was over, except Earl Weaver. He was telling four umpires with a combined total of 28 years of Major League experience that they did not know the rules.

"A runner does not get three bases on an overthrow," Weaver bellowed at Springstead and Larry Barnett. "Norris should have gone from first to third base, not home plate."

In the Cleveland radio booth, Joe Tait was saying, "Wait a minute. I don't think this game is over. Earl Weaver is talking to the umpires. I think they're going to bring the teams back on the field."

Weaver had checked the rule book and knew the umpires had blown rule 7:05 (g).

"It says right in the book, the guy only gets two bases," insisted Weaver.

The umpires conferred, then agreed with Earl. The teams returned to the field. Even Indians manager Jeff Torborg understood Weaver's reasoning.

"When the game ended, it flashed through my mind that something was not quite right," said Torborg. "But the game was over according to the umpires and I was not about to question a victory."

"Earl is 100% right," Springstead told Torborg. "We've got to continue the game and Norris goes back to third base."

Torborg did not argue.

So the Indians and Orioles were called back into action.

"I was in the locker room with my pants off and on my second piece of chicken when they said we were playing again," recalled Brooks Robinson.

The Indians failed to drive in Norris from third. In the tenth inning Baltimore scored twice and went on to take a 5–3 victory in a game everyone except Earl Weaver thought they had lost.

"When I first told Springstead about the two bases on the overthrow, he said something to me about the position of the runners," said Weaver. "I told him that had nothing to do with it."

Suddenly, Springstead had changed his tone, telling Weaver he was "150% right."

"I thought he was kidding," said Weaver. "I was going to protest the game for the second time. (Earlier, Earl had complained about a call on an interference play.) But they never would have upheld those protests. I talked to (American League President) Lee MacPhail about the situation and he agreed that the umpires had been 100% wrong. But I don't think the umpires should be fined. I just think they should try to do a better job."

Doing a better job—that is all Weaver maintains is behind his outbursts. When he says, "The umpires always give Carl Yastrzemski five strikes," he says he means it. "They won't call the guy out on good pitches. A good pitch is a strike no matter who is batting."

There is far more to it than that. It is a combination of theatrics, intimidation, and frustration. Weaver and Palmer are never closer than when they work over a home plate umpire. Palmer throws a pitch near the corner that he feels is a strike. The umpire disagrees. Palmer peers in at him. From the dugout, Weaver is screaming, demanding that the idiot behind the plate wake up. Palmer is going into the Hall of Fame. He knows what a strike is. Often this method is a winner. If Yastrzemski gets five strikes in every at bat in Fenway Park, Palmer receives an extra inch or two on the plate while hurling in Baltimore.

Earl also is cunning. On one occasion in which the Orioles were playing the White Sox, Weaver was convinced home plate umpire Larry McCoy simply did not have a clue as to what was a ball or what was a strike. Earl walked to the mound to talk with pitcher Rudy May and catcher Dave Skaggs.

"Did he miss those pitches?" Weaver shouted to Skaggs, who was standing next to him.

"I think he missed one, maybe two," replied Skaggs.

The exchange was loud enough for McCoy to hear. McCoy could not resist. He walked to the mound and Weaver was ready for him.

"Are you taking the pitcher out?" asked McCoy.

"No, I'm not taking the pitcher out," said Weaver. "I'm talking to my players and I plan to stay here."

McCoy then gave Earl the huge, windmill "You're out" gesture with his arm.

"So you think I'm out?" asked Weaver. "Well, I'll tell you something, You're the one who is out. I talked to Lee MacPhail and you're not working tomorrow's game."

Then Earl gave McCoy an ejection motion of his own.

After the game, Earl explained his plan. "McCoy didn't know it, but I had heard he was not going to be back in Chicago the next day, anyway. I wasn't supposed to know he was leaving. So when I told him he was out, he looked at me funny. He was stunned. He was wondering. I had him thinking. It took him a long time to get it."

Earl is not a big winner with umpires. No one is. The fact that he has emerged on top in even a handful of instances is astounding. But Weaver puts on a good show.

Perhaps his best show took place June 18, 1979 in Cleveland, a day after the famed "Father's Day" incident in which Weaver told Palmer to "grow up." In Cleveland, it was "Grandstand Manager's Night," a promotion by the *Cleveland Plain Dealer* in which the newspaper gave out free tickets to fans who expressed their opinions on various baseball topics in the paper. For seven innings the 34,333 fans were busy watching runners from both teams cross the plate. The Orioles carried a 7–6 lead into the eighth inning. Indians' Mike Hargrove led off with a base hit. Then Dave Rosello bunted in front of home plate. Baltimore catcher Rick Dempsey bolted after the roller and bumped into Rosello, who was running to first.

"Interference," Weaver screamed from the dugout. "The runner is out." Instead, Rosello was safe at first and home plate

umpire Larry Barnett explained that he saw no violation of the
rule.

Weaver was stunned by what he felt was the umpire's limitless
stupidity. As he ran from the dugout he was in a rage. His face was
red, his voice a loud screech, like the sound coming from a car
making a sudden stop. He went from one umpire to another,
waving his arms. He wanted to appeal straight to the Supreme
Court, to St. Peter, even the Almighty. Someone, somewhere
had to give him justice, he said.

"It's in black and white," said Weaver. "The rule on interference is clear. It is right in the book and it covers a play just like
this."

The umpires would have none of it.

When words failed him, Weaver dashed back to the dugout.
He returned to the diamond with a rulebook. He had it open to
the interference rule and began showing the page to Barnett. The
umpire would not look at it. Instead, he ejected Weaver.

That was it. Earl's blood pressure had risen higher than the
Empire State Building.

"If the rulebook doesn't mean anything, then let's tear it up,"
Earl told the umpires. "If we're not going to play by the rules,
there is no sense having a book."

Slowly, he began ripping pages out of the rulebook and tossing
them in the air. They floated down on the manager and umpires
like confetti. Soon the ground was littered with the rulebook.
Earl then noticed a large piece of paper near the pitchers mound.
He picked it up and carried it to the pitcher's rubber. There, at
the highest point of the field, he shredded the last bit of the
rulebook, then strutted off the diamond to a standing ovation
from the fans and scribes in the press box. He tipped his cap to the
crowd. Players in both dugouts were doubled over with laughter.

The Orioles were 8–7 winners, and after the game Weaver
gave a blow-by-blow description of his performance. He was like
a golfer verbally replaying a round, making sure not to neglect a
single detail. He was reveling in the attention. The applause still
had him on one of those special highs experienced only by people
in the public eye.

"There ain't no rule in the rulebook that says you can't take a
rulebook on the field. You guys get all that down?" Weaver asked
the press. "I told them guys they made the wrong call. I told them

it was in black and white. They wouldn't look at it so I ripped it up and it was all over the field in black and white."

Then Weaver critiqued the umpires as if he were a New York Times theatre reviewer.

"That Jim Evans, he gets boiling mad faster than any ump around. At least he don't carry a grudge from one series to another. Then there's Barnett. He made a call just like this in the 1975 World Series. Ed Armbrister bunted the ball and he collided with Carlton Fisk. Barnett didn't call interference then. I told him I almost kicked in my television set the first time he blew the call. They [umpires] are just gonna get worse now. They'll get us so bad. We won and it was brutal. But this was some game. Those "Grandstand Managers" really saw some managing. I could see all this coming in the fifth inning. That is when Eddie Murray got tossed out for arguing a pickoff play. Hell, that was the first time Eddie was run out of a big league game. From there, it just got worse. You know, those umps don't even have rulebooks on the field. I'm thinking about sending my lineup to the plate in a rulebook tomorrow so they'll have one."

Earl did not pull his rulebook trick the next day. But he received several copies through the mail when he arrived at the park.

"The first one I got was from (Indians General Manager) Phil Seghi," said Weaver. "He should have put some money in it because I'm bringing in an extra couple thousand people to see if I get tossed out again."

In 1979, Weaver went on one of the most renowned rampages in his career. He was ejected six times in seven weeks, starting with the rulebook shredding in Cleveland.

A month after the rulebook incident, the Orioles were playing in Oakland. On hand were umpires Larry Barnett, Rich Garcia, Jim Evans, and Fred Spenn—the same crew present for Weaver's Oscar-winning performance in Cleveland. This time nothing was ripped apart and the wildest guy on the field was Baltimore reliever Sammy Stewart.

It all began in the eighth inning. The Orioles had a 6–4 lead. Stewart hit leadoff batter Jim Essian in the ribs with a pitch. One hitter later, he nailed Oakland's Jeff Newman in the hand with another errant fastball. Out of the dugout bolted Weaver, insisting the pitch did not hit Newman's hand.

"It got his bat," repeated Weaver. "It's a foul fall, a strike. He don't get first."

This went on for four or five minutes before Garcia threw Earl out. Some say Earl earned the ejection by calling Garcia a "dog." Meanwhile, Newman was in pain because of Stewart's pitch. He left the game and outfielder Larry Murray was imported from the bullpen to pinch run for him. As the change took place, Stewart was warming up. Suddenly, first base umpire Jim Evans ran to the mound and ordered Stewart to stop throwing. Once again, Weaver, who was about to leave the premises, dashed out of the dugout. He was shaking his head. He was stomping a circle. He was waving his finger. He was screaming at Evans, wondering aloud how God in Heaven could have created someone so mis-guided. On and on it went. Eventually, Murray took over for Newman at first base and Weaver departed.

As play resumed, an Oriole with his jacket pulled up around his ears left the dugout and walked behind the plate and into the Birds' clubhouse. At a quick glance it looked like Weaver.

After a few pitches, Oakland Manager Jim Marshall was on the field.

"Weaver's in the bathroom," Marshall said while pointing to the Orioles' dugout.

The umpires did not move.

"You guys are going to have to carry me bodily off the field unless you get Weaver out of the bathroom," said Marshall.

Two of the umpires cautiously proceeded to the O's dugout. They opened the door of the one-room bathroom and found Weaver standing there, a cigarette dangling from his lips. This time, the umpires made sure Weaver was the man in the Balti-more jacket walking behind home plate and into the clubhouse. Earlier, Terry Crowley had served as the decoy. After the game, Weaver was ready for the press.

"I was in the bathroom because of the calls they made out there," said Weaver. "The calls made me sick to my stomach. I was throwing up in the john. When they came over to the dug-out and asked me what I was doing, I told them they made me throw up."

"That's interesting," said umpire Larry Barnett. "I have never seen anyone throw up with a cigarette in his mouth before."

"I have been thrown out of a lot of places," said Weaver. "But never a bathroom. I had to protest this game. Them guys just don't know the rules. Evans tried to stop a pitcher from warming up during a delay in the game. There ain't no rule in the book about that. Let them find one. They won't because there ain't one. You want to know something about these guys? Not one of them knows a thing about baseball. Nothing. In fact, they were still talking about what happened in Cleveland. They brought up the rulebook thing. In essence, they said they were going to stick it to us. Listen, you know what is in these guys' hearts. You know what kind of Christians they are."

The umpires also had their fill of Weaver.

"Earl Weaver is the Son of Sam of baseball," said Jim Evans. "If Earl is the game's resident genius (as a *Sports Illustrated* cover claimed), then the Son of Sam was a genius with a rifle."

When Earl was kicked out of the bathroom, Evans and Barnett had applauded with the fans as he left the field.

"It was a show," explained Evans. "You clap for clowns in a circus. Weaver is like a little kid. He tries to manipulate the umpires. When one of his tactics doesn't work, he gets mad. He doesn't like getting his wrists slapped." The next day, when Weaver carried the lineup card to home plate, he had a message for Evans.

"I didn't know you knew my father," said Weaver.

"Who?" asked Evans.

"You know, Sam," said Weaver. "The Son of Sam? Remember?"

Evans grumbled and the game went on without a conflict. That is often the case after an ejection. Seldom does Weaver put on two straight days of tirades. Usually, the first one and his post-game charges of the umpires "wanting to stick it to us," serve their purpose—to make the umpires bear down and pay attention. Earl knows his actions challenge them on a professional level to put personalities aside to maintain a detached attitude. In fact, some umpires are so bent on displaying their objectivity that they give the Orioles the benefit of the doubt just to demonstrate they have nothing against Weaver. While he never admits it, this is often behind Weaver's actions.

Early in his big league career, Earl was more expansive in talking about his reactions to umpires.

Frank Umont was the umpire who had once ejected Earl for

smoking in the dugout, and he became one of Earl's favorite targets. During a game in 1970 when Umont called a strike on Frank Robinson, the Oriole could not believe it. Umont could not believe Robinson would disagree with a call that seemed so obvious to the umpire. In the dugout, Weaver could not believe any of it, expecially when Umont banished Robinson. Soon Weaver was on the scene, berating the umpire. Then he returned to the dugout only to grow angry and come out again.

"I thought about getting thrown out real early in the game to get a well-umpired game out of Umont," said Weaver.

"I don't know why Earl had to put on a show, and he kept up the abuse when he went back to the dugout," said Umont. "When he came out to home plate again, I listened to him for a while and told him he had had his say. I wanted him to go back to the dugout, but he wouldn't. Then, he says something like now that he has been thrown out, why don't I let Robinson back in? Can you believe that? He thinks he's a big league manager. He wants respect, but if he acts like a child, he is not going to get it."

There have been over 80 run-ins with umpires, but some of Weaver's best are:

• In a 1973 game with Cleveland when Orioles' outfielder Paul Blair struck out, Indians' catcher Alan Ashby dropped the ball and Blair ran to first. Meanwhile, the Indians had left the field because they thought Blair was the last out of the inning. No one but Weaver saw Ashby drop the ball. Weaver charged on the field. He went from umpire to umpire, appealing his case. He was flapping his arms. He was kicking dirt.

"Four umpires and none of you guys saw him drop the ball," Weaver bellowed, picking up a handful of dirt and tossing it in the air. As a result, the umpires went into a huddle and changed their decision—Ashby had indeed dropped the ball, and Blair was safe at first. When Earl noticed the new ruling, he applauded them. He walked over to umpires Bill Kunkel and Marty Springstead and with a grand arm gesture, "threw both of them out of the game." Weaver was immediately ejected and he strutted off the field to a standing ovation.

"Sure I threw them out," Weaver told the *Baltimore Evening Sun's* Bill Tanton. "They blew the call. They should have been thrown out, not me. That's what gets managers thrown out of games, stuff like that. I go out to argue a call; it turns out I'm right. They have four guys out there and none of them can get the call straight. They should play with two umpires and two alternates."

• In another game with Cleveland in 1973, Earl felt the umpires did not know when a check swing constituted a strike. Ray Fosse was batting for the Indians and he waved at a 2 ball, 2 strike pitch. Weaver yelled out that it was strike three. Home plate umpire Larry Barnett had other ideas. It was a ball, proclaimed Barnett. On the next pitch, Fosse connected for a two-run homer. As he rounded the bases, Weaver flung a helmet onto the field and was immediately ejected.

"Throwing equipment on the field brings an automatic ejection," said Barnett.

"I didn't mean to do it," rationalized Weaver. "When he hit the homer, I picked up some bats and gave them a fling. The helmet was on top of them and it flew onto the field. I didn't know it went on the field until the umpire told me I was gone."

• During a 1978 game with the Angels, Earl was banished for throwing his cap. He had an explanation for this, too.

Early in the game, California pitcher Paul Hartzell had flung his cap to the ground in disgust when he thought the umpires blew a double play call. Weaver claimed Hartsell should have been ejected for "throwing equipment." The umpires disagreed.

Later in the contest, Weaver was upset when umpire Rich Garcia made a decision against the Birds. Earl grabbed his cap and tossed it to the dugout floor. Garcia saw the gesture and ejected Weaver. Earl roared out of the dugout, waving his finger in Garcia's face, and Garcia claimed that Weaver had poked him twice. Earl demanded an explanation of why Hartzell could throw a cap and he couldn't. Garcia said there was more to Weaver's ejection than the cap. The debate continued long after Earl left the field and the game had ended.

Earl replied that the umpires should be given a test to determine their competency. He said the Orioles were going to take this to court, "go the due process route. I've got a lawyer, Russell J. White, in case anything happens."

Weaver continued his raving to the Baltimore press: " I hope (American League President) Lee MacPhail knows one guy can throw his hat in the middle of the field before 23,000 witnesses and another can't do it in the confines of the dugout. It's a double standard. Even women have equal rights in this country. This just isn't the American way and it is supposed to be the national pastime. I wish MacPhail would give me a list of people who are allowed to throw their hats....I did not poke Garcia, either. [umpires] are born liars. Maybe they learn to lie in umpire school."

When umpire Ron Luciano came into the dispute to assist Garcia, Weaver told him, "Get out of here, no one will believe you. You're a clown."

Although Weaver usually knows how hard to push umpires before backing off, three times he has stepped over the fine line of baseball decorum and wound up with a suspension. Earl refuses to recognize a suspension or fine. He threatened to take Lee MacPhail and the Baltimore Orioles to court when he was fined around $250 for arguing a balk call in 1978. Of course Earl never did and the fine was quietly paid, but he will never admit it.

Though a fine can be handled behind the scenes with a check to the American League office, suspensions are another matter.

The first occurred in 1976. Palmer and Weaver both were a part of the league action, although what led to their penalties did not take place in the same game.

Palmer drew a $500 fine for admitting he had thrown a retaliatory pitch at the Yankees' Mickey Rivers. It was a payback for Doc Ellis, who had, earlier in the game, plunked the Orioles Reggie Jackson in the skull and sent him to the hospital with a minor head injury. In baseball, an eye-for-an-eye intellect often prevails. When a batter is hit, his teammates expect their pitcher to take action against the other team. As in most sports, intimidation plays a strong role in baseball. When Jackson went down, Palmer knew he had to do something. No one said anything to him, and Weaver never directs a pitcher to throw at a batter. Though Palmer's beanball missed Rivers, it served the purpose. It sent a message to the Yankees. If Ellis or any other New York pitcher was going to nail a Baltimore batter, the Orioles would reply in kind.

After the game, Ellis denied he had purposely hit Jackson. On the other hand, the outspoken and ever-honest Palmer admitted his actions.

"I did it to protect my teammates," said Palmer. "I don't find any great delight in hitting batters. I don't believe any pitcher does, except when it is to keep other pitchers from throwing at your hitters."

The American League did not see it that way. They fined Palmer $500, mostly for owning up to his deed. Because Ellis would not say he had intentionally dented Jackson's head, he was given a not guilty verdict. So much for truthfulness in baseball.

On the same day Palmer's fine was announced, the American League suspended Weaver. This took place because of a dispute with umpire Dale Ford. Ford had called Lee May out on strikes then ejected the Orioles' first baseman for prolonged complaints. Weaver rushed from the dugout and was immediately thrown out. Managers are not permitted to argue ball or strike calls on the field. Weaver claimed he was just "trying to protect May. I wanted Ford to throw me out, not Lee."

When Ford scored his double play by exiling May and Weaver, Earl was especially angry. He turned his cap around like a catcher's, so the beak would not bang the umpire in the face during their nose-to-nose argument. Earl was waving his fingers in Ford's face, perilously close to the umpire's lips. Both men said contact was made.

In his report to the American League office, Ford stated Weaver cut his lips by striking him with two of his fingers. Touching an umpire usually brings a suspension and this was no exception. Earl was ordered to sit out three games. In his defense, Weaver said Ford forced the issue. Furthermore, Earl maintained he did not intentionally make contact with Ford. The American League office ruled against Weaver.

The most famous suspension of Weaver's career was in late August of 1979. It concluded his string of six ejections in seven weeks. The Orioles were in Chicago and they had been "rained out" for two games even though the skies were sunny. Earlier in the week, it had poured for a few days. Then, White Sox Owner Bill Veeck had promoted a rock concert at Comiskey Park. Between the music fans, the rain and the energy created by *Pablo Cruise*, the outfield had been transformed into the surface of the moon. As the Orioles prepared to meet the White Sox, the diamond was too torn up for the following good weather to help. So the first two games of the three-day series were postponed.

On the third day, a Sunday, they went ahead with a dou-

bleheader, but not without protests from Weaver and players
from both teams. Weaver called the field . . . "a safety hazard,"
and said, "we should be awarded the whole series on a forfeit. The
Cubs played in town this week and were not rained out. The
condition of the field is the fault of the White Sox, not the
elements."

The O's held a meeting and voted unanimously that the field
was "unplayable." Later, a number of Orioles and White Sox
players discussed the situation and determined that American
League President Lee MacPhail and the umpires should be held
responsible if any athlete was injured. MacPhail and the umpires
had made the decision to go ahead and play. The players drew up
a statement and it was signed by player representatives from both
teams.

The umpires witnessed it all and Weaver repeated his protest
about the field. He said the only reason the Orioles agreed to play
was that MacPhail threatened any team not taking part with a
forfeit. Under orders from Bill Veeck, White Sox Manager Tony
LaRussa "protested Weaver's protest."

At home plate was Ron Luciano, Earl's foremost adversary
among umpires. The two men had begun arguing in the Eastern
League. They carried the fight to the International League and to
the American League. The relationship had degenerated with
each passing year. In 1977, Luciano was quoted as saying, "I hate
Earl Weaver, and I hope any team wins but Weaver's."

That's pretty strong stuff from an umpire, who is supposed to
be an unbiased arbiter. The American League required Luciano
to make a public apology to Weaver. He did. Also, Luciano was
not assigned to any Orioles games for two years until that Sunday
in Chicago in 1979.

In the interim Weaver often spoke of Luciano. He seemed to
be waiting for the time when they would meet again.

Luciano was behind the plate in the first game and the Birds
had built a 10–5 lead after four innings. In the fifth, Luciano
called Baltimore third baseman Doug DeCinces out on a pitch.

"It was outside and six inches low," said DeCinces.

Weaver stepped out of the dugout and held his hands above his
head, pleading for divine intervention. The manager did not say a

word, but Luciano ejected him. The umpire did it with an unobtrusive point of a finger.

"I didn't even know he threw me out" said Weaver. "I was just trying to make sure DeCinces did not get thrown out. I didn't know I got it until I asked him."

Weaver's exchange with Luciano was extremely subdued. Then Earl had White Sox public address announcer Bob Finnigan read the following statement to the 25,605 fans:

"Ladies and gentlemen, Earl Weaver is protesting today's game on the grounds of the umpire's integrity."

"I exploded when I heard that," said MacPhail, who was in the stands. "Earl can't do that. He can't publicly question the integrity of the umpires. What does that mean? Luciano's dishonest?"

Weaver claimed Luciano's remarks of a few years ago illustrated a bias. MacPhail would not even listen, and he suspended Earl for three games.

"We tried to keep Luciano and Weaver apart," said MacPhail. "But these things can't go on forever. This was a very serious thing to make public. It is one thing to tell it to the writers after a game and it is another to have it broadcast to 25,000 people."

MacPhail's logic seems a bit distorted. Why would it be all right to express these sentiments to the media (who will carry the message to millions of fans) and not to those in the park?

"We've tried to tolerate Weaver's actions this year, but I cannot stand Earl making a public comment like that" MacPhail stated.

Earl was cavalier about his suspension.

"It don't bother me none," he said. "I ain't gonna pay attention to it. I might take a couple days off because Luciano has upset my nerves, but I ain't suspended. I'm not sure what I'm gonna do in the next couple days. Maybe I'll go to my house in Miami. Maybe I'll sit in the press box. Maybe I'll even be in the dugout bathroom. I think I'll stay around and root for the team. What do you expect me to do, root against us like Luciano does?"

Weaver went on about his right to question Luciano's integrity.

"That's the first time I ever got tossed out without saying a word," said Weaver. "All I did was raise my hands. Look, I don't care what the umpires say or think about me. I just don't want them rooting against us. I know Luciano is, I just hope that he's not betting against us."

Weaver made no effort to appeal his suspension. "The guy I'd appeal to is MacPhail and he suspended me. It don't look like I'd have much of a chance."

The next day, Earl continued his alleged ignorance of his penalty as the Orioles prepared for a doubleheader in Minnesota.

"Who's suspended?" he asked. "I don't believe in fines or suspensions. I'm just taking a few days off. You know, that experience with Luciano yesterday has made me very nervous. I need some rest. I have nightmares. I see myself walking up to home plate with the lineup card and there are four umpires standing there and all of them are Ron Luciano."

Earl obviously had his act down pat. He was determined not to let the American League get the best of him. As always, he wanted the last word.

"The amazing thing about Earl is that he always makes the best of the worst situations," said the team's traveling secretary, Phil Itzoe. "When the team is going lousy or he's having a tough time, he's up. When things are great, he looks for things to complain about."

According to the rules, a manager under suspension can go to the game, but he cannot be in the dugout or clubhouse once play starts. When the press arrived at the park, Earl was writing out his lineup.

"You guys see me doing this?" Earl asked. "Well, it's not my lineup. It's Cal's [coach Cal Ripken's]. He made it out. I'm just copying it."

Sure, Earl.

"Hey, we got a new system here. We're going to use what I call the 'college of managers.' No one coach is in charge. They'll confer on decisions and they each have been assigned an umpire to argue with."

Hearing this Weaver comment, John Lowenstein said, "Earl is smart. This college of managers guarantees that no one gets the credit while he's gone. Speaking of colleges, when do you think there will be a manager and coaching staff who all graduated from college?"

The players enjoyed Weaver's new status. Pat Kelly and Eddie Murray sang, "No more Weaver tonight," from a corner of the clubhouse.

"I need a ticket to get in tonight," Weaver shouted at his players. "Who's going to leave me one so the umpires don't think I'm hiding in the bathroom or something?"

"I'll leave you one," said Terry Crowley. "How much does a ticket to France cost?"

Weaver spent the Oriole–Twins doubleheader seated behind home plate. He wore a sport shirt. At his side were scouts Jim Russo and Bill Werle. Russo and Werle would give signs to third base coach Ripken while Weaver sat back innocently. After the 4–3 loss in the opener, there must have been some mix-up because Weaver closed the clubhouse to reporters. That was a first for him. In the second game, Palmer beat the Twins, 5–1.

"I guess this just goes to show that we're a .500 team without Earl," said Palmer after the split. "It was very peaceful in the dugout. No second guessing or other distractions with Earl not there. When he's 30 rows up in the seats, it's hard to hear. I did hear him whistle at me and I think he yelled something about throwing my slider more."

On the bus back to the hotel after the game, Weaver said, "Maybe I'll rest again tomorrow. Besides, a lot of people say I don't do anything around here, so I just did what I usually do . . . watched the game."

Reporters asked Weaver, the scouts, and the coaches about the possibility of signals being sent from the manager. There were denials all around until someone mentioned to Russo that he held his hands above his head quite a bit.

"Well, there was the fat guy in front of me," said Russo. "And Ripken had a hard time seeing me."

Guilty as charged.

Weaver was obviously enjoying his suspension . . . ah . . . "mini-vacation" as he called it. He knew he was supposed to sit out three games. Two were used up the first day and another doubleheader was on tap. This created an interesting question.

"Do I sit out the first game or the second?" asked Weaver.

Earl and umpire Marty Springstead had a long discussion on this matter. The debate went on *ad nauseam*. First, Springstead ruled Weaver could suit up for the first contest, but not the second. Then the American League office called and declared Weaver must miss three straight games. Hence, he was out for the first and in for the second. Hearing this, Earl proclaimed he would skip them both. His mind was churning and he blurted out a few possibilities designed to send the umpires scurrying for their rulebooks.

"I think I'll sit in the stands with a walkie-talkie and have John Lowenstein in the dugout wearing earphones," said Weaver. "The Twins will go nuts and protest. The umpires will check Lowenstein's earphones and expect to hear my voice. Instead, they will get music . . . Or maybe I'll sit in the dugout, but not in uniform. Connie Mack did that for 50 years when he managed the Philadelphia A's, why not me?"

The umpires had an answer for the second suggestion. Earl must wear a uniform to be in the dugout. He could go into the dugout *runway* in street clothes, but only during the second game. Weaver remained in the stands. The Orioles won a doubleheader and Earl came up with another wrinkle.

"Now that the suspension is over, I don't know if I'll be in uniform or not. I am considering legal action against Luciano. He has caused me grief. He hurt my sex life."

The statement about Earl's bedroom activities made a headline in the *St. Paul Dispatch*. It read: UMPIRE UPSETS WEAVER'S SEX LIFE.

Seeing the newspaper, Earl quickly amended his statement to, "I meant it will hurt my sex life when I get home."

The Orioles were beginning to wonder if Earl's ego had finally gone on an unstoppable rampage. His actions were distracting attention from the club, which deserved praise for its fine performances. Either Earl figured this out, or was informed of it by Orioles General Manager Hank Peters. As a result, he was back in uniform when he was supposed to be, and he was not ejected for the remainder of 1979.

Earl has been suspended two other times, but they lacked the bizarreness of his 1979 stunts.

In 1980, Weaver again stepped out of bounds according to the American League. The Orioles were hosting the Yankees. Pat Kelly was called out on a checked swing and Weaver began throwing things on the field. Out of the dugout came three gloves, several towels and other items. Umpires Steve Palermo and Rich Garcia ejected Earl.

"They never told me I was out," Earl said later, but he did hide in the dugout runway anyway.

Next inning, New York's Eric Soderholm homered. That put the Yankees in front, 4-1, in the eighth, and it ignited Weaver. He dashed out of the runway, up the dugout steps and onto the field. Garcia moved toward the dugout to tell Earl that he had already been thrown out. Weaver went up to Garcia and started a nose-to-nose argument. Palermo joined the fight, as did umpire Dale Ford. Weaver turned to each of them to plead his case. When he received no satisfaction, he walked to second base and said he would not move until justice was rendered. Palermo attempted to dissuade him. It was futile, so the umpire returned to home plate and bent over to dust it off with his whisk broom. As Palermo was working on the plate, he discovered Weaver right behind him. It appeared Earl might kick him in the rear. Suddenly, he booted dirt through Palermo's legs. The plate was covered and Earl departed.

"When I was out there, I was thinking about how much time I had before I was in serious trouble," said Weaver. "I was hoping Palermo would take out his watch and tell me how much time I had. In the minors, they did that to Grover Reisinger, saying he had one minute left. He asked the umpire for the watch. When the ump gave it to him, he threw it out of the park. That's what I wanted to do to Palermo."

It was great theatre for everyone except the umpires and Lee MacPhail. Again, Weaver was suspended for three games. Mac-Phail said Earl "made physical contact with Garcia, hitting him in the eye with his cap."

Earl appealed this ruling and lost. He was out for three days with little fanfare.

Weaver is probably the only manager to be suspended in spring training. It all started because, "The umpires were messing around with the rules again," according to Earl.

The situation was this:

Baltimore was playing Kansas City on March 19, 1981. It was just another exhibition game. Ex-Oriole Coach and Royals Manager Jim Frey made several lineup changes. During the regular season, it is an umpire's duty to present the opposing manager with the substitutions and the official batting order. Rookie umpire Mark Johnson decided he could skip this procedure because it was a spring game.

Weaver had other ideas.

He was out on the field, demanding the new lineup and talking about rule 3:03, which states the umpire must notify the manager if more than on change is made.

"I wanted the names, positions and the batting order," Weaver explained.

"This is a spring game, it doesn't mean anything," replied Johnson.

"How am I supposed to know if somebody is batting out of order?" asked Weaver. "I've been managing 34 years and I want to know the names of everybody in the lineup because we keep charts, even in the spring. Those charts could be helpful. I won't continue the game unless I get the lineup. You may think these games don't mean anything, but people in the stands paid money to see them so they must think they're important."

Vic Voltaggio was the umpire crew chief. He backed Johnson.

"What does Voltaggio know?" asked Weaver. "He was one of the guys who let everybody run off the field in Cleveland when the game wasn't over."

Realizing no one was listening to him, Earl pulled the Orioles off the field. MacPhail quickly suspended Earl, even though he agreed the Oriole manager was correct.

"Twice Earl has taken his team off the field," said MacPhail. "He also did it in Toronto in 1977 and I don't recall any other manager doing it. There is no place in the game for this kind of thing."

Earl treated this suspension like all the others.

"What suspension," he said, using a familiar line. "I think I'll have a three-day sit out. Maybe I'll get a little more productivity out of the American League. It will be a form of protest in support of President Reagan. He wants more productivity and he wants to eliminate waste. I think everyone will agree with me in saying this is the stupidest thing done in baseball."

During his "sit out," Weaver watched minor league exhibition games. When he returned, he was presented with lineup changes. There also was a clear warning from the league office— Earl could not continue this type of action.

"I have fined Earl countless times and suspended him," said MacPhail. "Nothing helps. The Orioles are responsible for his actions. The next time he steps out of line, it will be a far more severe penalty."

Umpires and Weaver have been attacking and threatening each other in print for years. Their statements would fill volumes. Sometimes they are funny. Sometimes they are childish. Sometimes they are stupid. Always, they are insulting.

One time, Weaver blamed an Oriole loss on umpires who would not wait until it stopped raining. Naturally, the Birds were losing when the showers halted the contest.

"If the Orioles were ahead instead of behind when we stopped the game because of the weather, Earl would have been in the umpire's room 15 times asking us how long we planned to wait," said Marty Springstead. "If it isn't Earl's way, it isn't life. That's his way. He's got to have something to bitch about. When it rained, Earl wanted me to look under the tarpaulin and see how wet the infield was. Hell, I didn't have to look. But that's how he is."

While Springstead has ejected Weaver nine times, more than any other umpire, Earl's most heated feuds have been with Jim Evans and, again, Ron Luciano. Earl won't permit Luciano to forget his comment about hoping Weaver's team would lose every game. Even though Luciano has left the ball park for sports broadcasting, Earl occasionally brings up the subject. Both men used to send each other into a frenzy. Weaver would complain that Luciano was once a good umpire but had faltered miserably as media attention came his way, and that he was acting as though he was bigger than the game and its players—a mortal sin for an umpire. This was not only Earl's view, but that of most of the American League. These words Luciano did not like to hear, especially from Weaver. The two men seemed to bring out the worst in each other.

"Earl acts like he wants everything," Luciano once said. "He even wants you to cheat for him. He would stand there, jawing at you. He'd be kicking dirt on you, like a dog burying a bone. Pretty soon, you were underground from the ankles down. He can be very obnoxious. Every umpire has an Earl Weaver. We went back to Class AA in Reading. I threw him out in the first four games I had him. He never got past the fourth inning. In the fifth game, he brought the lineup card out and asked me if I was going to be as shitty as I was the first four nights. I told him he was not going to find out and threw him out again."

"Once you've ejected Earl, he is like the child who can't accept authority," Larry Barnett has said. "He goes through the whole list of things you have done to him. He's a historian. I've never seen anything funny about him except when he once slipped coming out of the dugout."

"Weaver is the ayatollah of the 1980s," according to umpire Nick Bremigan.

Jim Evans, who called Earl "baseball's Son of Sam," heated up their war in 1975. In a game against the Angels, Evans tossed out coaches Jim Frey, Billy Hunter, DH Tommy Davis, and Weaver. The area of contention was several ball and strike calls on Davis.

"Evans owes me an apology," Weaver told the *Baltimore Morning Sun's* Ken Nigro. "He provoked the whole thing. I feel I am the damaged party. It was a typical Evans game with both sides hollering at him all night. He is full of snide remarks. He is like your own son talking back to you. I don't want anybody's job, but the quicker he is gone the better it will be for the American League."

"Weaver never has been a fair manager," Evans told Nigro. "He is always looking for a crutch. He's a cheerleader type and he hollers at his players like a little league coach . . . All the fines and suspensions we've had is indicative of our society. There is no respect for authority and it has carried over to baseball. Some managers are always looking for a crutch and they try to play the intimidation game. They try to put the monkey on your back. It seems to me managers and players can get away with things that an umpire would be fired for in a minute."

There is a famous story about the subject of vision.

"You see this eye," Evans once said to Weaver, pointing to one of his own eyes. "It's insured for $10,000." Then, Evans pointed to his other eye and repeated the sentence.

Earl looked at him and said, "So what did you do with the insurance money?"

That earned Weaver another trip to the dressing room.

Umpires have said Weaver acts like a lunatic. They say he has no control. Others suggest everything he does is calculated. All feel he steps out of bounds.

Steve Palermo holds this opinion, too. Palermo is relatively young and is sensitive about it. Any mention of age will get you the thumb. So you can imagine what Palermo thinks when he hears Earl saying, "The kid is still wet behind the ears. It is young guys like him that make me glad I'm getting out of the game in a couple years. They're ruining the game I spent my life in. You can't believe this guy. He lies. He's just a young punk. He has a chip on his shoulder."

"If I have a chip on my shoulder, Earl has a block of granite on his," said Palermo. "Look, he is just a clown under the guise of a manager. He's a pest. All umpires have more trouble with him than anyone else. All the run-ins are with Weaver and that should say something about his integrity. He's an insult to baseball and I'll be around longer than he will."

Umpires seem to have two theories about handling Weaver. One is that when he starts to mouth off, eject him immediately. Eliminate him for the rest of the game. The other is to try and keep him in the game as long as possible. Most of his base stealing, rulebook ripping, and finger pointing activities occur after he receives the thumb. While still in the game, he is at least under some control.

Many wonder if all this bickering with umpires helps the Orioles.

"All I can say is we had a game lost in Cleveland until I talked to the umpires. Then, they brought the teams back on the field and we won," said Weaver.

"Earl will stand up for you," said Ken Singleton. "He always tells us not to get thrown out, he will. He says he needs us in the game to hit a homer in the ninth inning and win it. Besides, he can run the team when he is out of the game. I remember a game in 1980 when we got beat 10–1 by the Yankees. We were terrible, but Earl got tossed. The next day, the papers were filled with stories about Earl and the umpires instead of how lousy we played. It took the heat off us. He may alienate some umpires, but he helps us, for the most part."

"The only manager who can get an umpire to change his mind is

Weaver," said Kansas City's Clint Hurdle. "I think he scares them."

"Guys like Billy Martin and Earl Weaver intimidate umpires," says the well-traveled Bobby Bonds. "They get more calls in favor of their teams because they are always on the umps."

"Umpires are human," said former Indians Manager Jeff Torborg. "When a manager continually works over an umpire, it is bound to have an effect. The thing about Weaver is not just that he is loud, but that he is a great baseball man."

"Everybody talks about me and the umpires," Says Weaver. "I don't go onto the field to put on a show. I'm out there because I'm mad or it looks like one of my players is going to get thrown out. The players win games, not me, so I want them on the field. Sometimes, I go out and put on a good show, but it happens as an afterthought when they throw me out. The main thing is the umpires sometimes don't know the rules or they are going to throw one of my players out."

"Earl's actions on the field are him," said veteran pitcher Rudy May. "He is not a put on. He says what he feels no matter if he is talking to the batboy or the team president. He'll never have a heart attack or ulcer because he doesn't keep anything inside."

The Weaver personality carries over into his team. Umpires say no club complains more than the Orioles. The players are not afraid to speak up because they know Earl will be right in the middle of the fight, prepared to carry their banner.

However, there is a side effect to all this that bothers Weaver.

"Whenever I get into a fight with an umpire or have a problem with Palmer, my parents call me up and say I'm embarrassing them," said Earl. "They ask me why I was in trouble again. Part of the problem is whenever they run my picture in the paper, I'm yelling at an umpire and looking like a jerk. They could take 50 pictures of me and 49 of them will have nothing to do with umpires, but you know which one they will pick!"

9

No Friend to Players

If the Orioles are on the road and Weaver is bitching about Bambi's Bombers, they must be in Milwaukee. Nothing will ever replace Kansas City as a baseball Armageddon in Weaver's heart, but Milwaukee during the managerial tenure of George Bamberger came close. Horrible things have happened to the Birds in Kansas City. In Milwaukee, their luck was just plain lousy. The Orioles opened the 1978 season in Milwaukee. After three games, they had been slugged for 40 runs and the Birds' pitchers had heaved seven wild pitches. For three years (1978–80), the Orioles first road series of the season began in Milwaukee. They went 1–9 in those contests, most of them as one-sided as a nuclear attack. To a team so dependent on and accustomed to stingy pitching, these outcomes were stunning. It is like Bjorn Borg discovering he cannot hit his first serve over the net or Tom Watson continually whacking his drives into sand traps.

No wonder Earl moans when he sees a trek to Milwaukee on his early-season schedule. By late summer, the aberration is over and the Baltimore pitchers usually hold baseball's most powerful club in check.

But April in Beer City is never a bargain. Often there is

145

snow. If not, there is rain. Sometimes, there is something falling from the sky that is between rain and snow. It is always cold, the kind of climate Weaver abhors. Earl is a creature of the sun and humidity. He finds nothing objectionable about sweating. His native St. Louis is almost tropical during the summer and so is Baltimore. In both places, your T-shirt will be soaked after a short July walk. Because Weaver owns a winter home in Miami, he avoids any possibility of snow. So Earl doesn't like the Milwaukee weather or its lineup—especially in April.

A typical Orioles–Brewers game in April was played on April 13, 1979. It was Good Friday, and Steve Stone, who is Jewish, jokingly made a remark about his being the sacrifice on this holy and symbolic day. Stone was right. Milwaukee was a 9–3 winner and he was smashed. But the way the Orioles lost served as a metaphor for all the disasters which have plagued them there.

The night began ominously when Ken Singleton was ejected for disagreeing with the home plate umpire. The regular umpires were on strike, so amateurs had been imported. The "umpire" who thumbed Singleton earned his regular living as a security guard. "This is the first time I have been thrown out and it was by a night watchman," Singleton said shaking his head after the game.

Later in the contest, Weaver bolted onto the field to offer a dissenting opinion on a call. The amateurs told Earl, yes, he was right but there was nothing they could do. The decision had to stand. Weaver was caught speechless. No one would fight with him. All he could do was walk off the field muttering to himself.

By the fourth inning, it was clear the catastrophe could not be reversed. Weaver was frustrated. "Not again," he said over and over. Then he saw Rick Dempsey picked off first base. Weaver refused to believe Dempsey would not slide back to the bag.

"Why didn't you slide?" he asked Dempsey as he returned to the dugout.

"I didn't need to," said Dempsey.

"What?" demanded Weaver.

"I didn't have to slide," explained Dempsey. "That is why I went back into the base standing up. I thought I could deflect the throw away."

"You thought wrong," said Weaver, who also mentioned a pop fly Dempsey failed to reach a few innings earlier. "Either you play the game the way I tell you to or get out."

Weaver then told Dave Skaggs to take over behind the plate for Dempsey.

Dempsey heard this and slammed down his catcher's mask.

Weaver grabbed the mask and threw it down.

Dempsey threw a shin guard against the dugout wall.

Weaver threw a shin guard against the wall.

Dempsey threw a batting helmet.

Weaver threw a batting helmet.

Dempsey stepped toward Weaver.

Weaver stepped toward Dempsey.

Then Coach Frank Robinson stepped between the two men and collared Dempsey. That ended the incident.

When the game was over, Weaver closed the clubhouse and held a 15-minute meeting. Later, Weaver and Dempsey were ready to face the press.

"They grabbed me before I could get to Earl," said Dempsey. "It was just one of those spur-of-the moment things. I apologized."

Because Earl was aware that most of the fans and the writers had seen the incident, he gave a blow-by-blow account. "If someone hadn't stopped us, we would have busted up the whole dugout," he said with a smile. "It all came down to the fact I wanted Rick to play the game my way. I'm the manager and I get blamed when he screws up. It is my job to make the guys do things right, and they are going to do it my way since I am responsible for their actions. If people around here are not going to do things my way, they won't play. It is as simple as that."

In one respect, Weaver does treat his players like umpires. When he feels like yelling, he shrieks at them. Seldom does he pass out compliments. Sometimes, the confrontations turn ugly.

Other times, they are simply comical. Always, they are misunderstood by someone—Earl, the player, the fans, or the press. Earl has often said he would like to be friends with his players. He muses that he would enjoy being Brooks Robinson, a guy almost everyone is fond of.

"More of his players like him than Earl thinks," said Toronto Blue Jays General Manager Pat Gillick. "Maybe he doesn't realize it, or maybe he feels that way because the players don't tell him their true feelings. But I played for Earl in the minors and I liked him. I think most of the guys who played for him did, too."

There are some Orioles who will never join the Earl Weaver fan club.

One is Doug DeCinces.

DeCinces did not have fate on his side. He reached the majors in time to play third base after Brooks Robinson retired. It was an impossible assignment, like being conductor of the Boston Pops after Arthur Fiedler. To make matters worse, DeCinces had three strikes against him. He did not come near Brooks in the field, at bat, or in personality. Brooks is headed for the Hall of Fame. When DeCinces quits, he will be recalled primarily as the Baltimore third baseman after Robinson. Brooks was an artist, DeCinces is a journeyman.

That does not make him a bad person or player. It only means he isn't Brooks Robinson. Some Oriole fans will never permit him to forget it, either. DeCinces also has a dark side. He ruffles at criticism and tends to brood in times of adversity. In this respect he is like many other players, but it further accents the fact he is not Brooks. DeCinces comes from a family of wealth. His father runs a successful construction business. Doug serves as a vice president. Many of his relatives work in show business. Several toiled behind the scenes on the old "Sky King" show. Like Palmer, DeCinces' background was refined and formal. It did little to prepare him for someone like Weaver.

So it has surprised no one that the two have clashed over the years. The first major incident was in 1978. The Orioles were playing Cleveland in the first game of a doubleheader. In this contest, DeCinces was used at second base. Weaver was riled when Doug did not throw home to prevent a run. Instead he threw to first base in a futile attempt to pull off a double play. That enabled Buddy Bell to score all the way from second base.

"You have got to be alert out there," Weaver said to DeCinces after the inning. DeCinces told Earl it wasn't his fault. Soon the two men were going for each other. They were separated by Pat Kelly.

"I felt I was 100% right on the play," DeCinces informed the *Baltimore Morning Sun's* Ken Nigro. "I'm not here to make trouble. When I get shown up in front of my teammates for something I didn't do, I'm not going to stand for it. I'm not going to be Weaver's scapegoat. It is his option to yell at me and it is my option to stand up for what I think is right. As soon as I had my say, he took me out of the game. Maybe I listen and listen and listen too much and it all builds up inside me. I think Earl second-guesses me a whole lot and I deserve it sometimes . . . Still, there is only so much belittling a person can take."

"Doug just got caught napping on the play," said Weaver. "There is nothing unusual about this. It happens between me and players like Jim Palmer or Bobby Grich or somebody else about ten times a year. I was so mad at the guy, I played him in the second game." Indeed, Weaver did and DeCinces drove in two runs to lead the Orioles to a victory.

The other spat was late in 1980. Trailing the first place Yankees by five games, the Orioles had 16 games left. DeCinces was frustrated. The Birds were on their way to a 100-victory season and that did not appear good enough to win the division.

"It looks like you can call in the dogs and spit on the fire because the hunt is over," DeCinces told Dan Shaughnessy of the *Washington Star*. The *Star* carried a story with DeCinces' picture and the headline "The Hunt is Over." Orioles Owner Edward Bennett Williams lives in Washington. He read the account and carried the story to the park the next day, showing it to both Weaver and DeCinces.

To his credit, DeCinces did not deny his remarks. But he did qualify the statement by explaining, "I said 'barring a miracle' . . . it was an unfortunate choice of words and I'm sorry."

Earl said he could not understand DeCinces.

"I have never heard that from a ballplayer in all my life," said Weaver. "It is the first time in my 33 years of baseball I have heard any player throw in the towel with three weeks to go. It's the most amazing thing I have ever heard. Only one player here is giving up. Twenty-four others, the coaches, and the manager still think we have a chance. I am not mad about what Doug said. He is entitled to his opinion. This is America and we have free speech. All I know is we have a lot of disappointed people around here."

It seemed Weaver's words served two purposes. One was to ignite his club and let them know any hint of negativism would not be tolerated. The other was a message to the Orioles fans and the club owner that Earl and his team were very serious about winning the pennant. It was a public relations ploy. DeCinces did not realize it, but he had set himself up as a scapegoat if the Orioles finished poorly. He would be forced to take the heat which otherwise would have been directed at Weaver, the front office or his teammates. And it was all because of a relatively harmless quote. As it turned out, DeCinces was right. Baltimore continued winning until the last day of the season, rolling up 100 victories. But so did New York. The Yankees finished with 103 triumphs. On the day DeCinces opened up, the hunt indeed was over. In baseball, you are not supposed to admit it. As was the case after the 1978 rumble in the dugout, Weaver continued to place DeCinces in the lineup. Doug held up his end by having a dynamic last three weeks.

Directly across the Orioles' clubhouse from DeCinces' locker was Kiko Garcia. Garcia and DeCinces had more in common than the same dressing room and uniform. Like DeCinces, Garcia was trying to replace a legend. But there was one difference. Garcia's ghost also shared the same quarters. As DeCinces was asked to take over for perhaps the greatest defensive third baseman in baseball history, Garcia's mission was to assume Mark Belanger's position. Few say Belanger is the premier glove ever to play shortstop. They simply say he is among the best in baseball history.

DeCinces joined the Orioles while Brooks was a member of the team, but Robinson's skills had eroded noticeably. The same was not true of Belanger. Mark was not hitting, but then he never did. Furthermore, Belanger often would enter the game as a defensive replacement for Garcia. Mark had not gained a pound since he became the Birds' shortstop in 1967. He still played the field with the same grace and remarkable steadiness of a 20-year-old. The reason Weaver elected to go with Garcia was his offense. Earl no longer had the hitting power of Frank Robinson, Brooks

Robinson, Boog Powell, and a few other heavy hitters who in the past had made up for Belanger's lifetime .229 batting average. Belanger was the same as always. It was Weaver's opinion that had changed. Oriole scouts had reported that Garcia had the raw talent to be a fine defensive shortstop.

That may have been the case, but Kiko Garcia floundered in the field. The fans knew he was no Belanger, and they wanted Mark. Belanger was "The Blade," skinny and smooth. If he touched a ball he had it in the middle of his child-size glove and was making a soft, chest high throw to the first baseman. Garcia was squat. He looked and moved like a wrestler. He had a tendency to flub the easiest ground balls, to the astonishment and dismay of the Orioles' fans.

Part of the reason for this was chronic back problems. Ironically, DeCinces also has been plagued with back pains. On several occasions it was suggested both men needed surgery and that they performed in great pain, but neither went under the surgeon's knife.

"Earl didn't make it easy for me with the Belanger situation," says Garcia. "Don't misunderstand, he didn't throw Mark up to me or anything like that. In fact, he never mentioned Mark. The fans brought it up a lot. I used to hear the stuff about Mark in my sleep. Mark was great to me. He helped me. But I won't be like him. No one ever will."

Garcia bottomed out by 1980. He batted .199 that year and threatened to take the front office to an arbitration hearing to gain a better contract. His defense was poor. That is why he was traded to Houston in the spring of 1981. Away from the Orioles, Garcia was able to place his time under Weaver in perspective.

"Playing for Earl is pretty hard," said Garcia. "He never said much to me. But he doesn't say much to anybody. He talks a lot to everyone in general, but it is rare to have a conversation with him. In 1980, I went to see him in his office to get things squared away. He said that when I hit I'd be in there, but that he'd take me out from the seventh inning on because Belanger was Hall of Fame material. I told him I was capable of playing the whole game, but he didn't see it that way.

"Don't get me wrong, Earl makes a lot of good moves," added Garcia. "But the team plays so well together that they make it work. The reason they win is the players, not Earl. Earl is amazing. From the first inning on, he is talking in the dugout. If the pitcher strikes out all three of our hitters in the first, he gets in a bad mood. He'll start asking over and over again how we could let this guy get us out. You get this negative feeling from the start. But I'll say this for the man, he doesn't talk behind your backs. If he has something to say to you, he says it. And Earl let's you say whatever is on your mind. You say it and then it is forgotten. That is healthy since you don't have to complain to your wife or coach. You go right to the man and let it out. People say Earl is funny. I don't see anything funny about Earl Weaver."

Another ex-Oriole who shares that opinion is Larry Harlow. Now a reserve outfielder with the Angels, Harlow was at the center of one of the disagreements between Earl and General Manager Hank Peters. Weaver critics also charge Harlow was one of the young players ruined by the manager.

"I'm a very quiet guy," said Harlow. "As for Earl, he doesn't say much to his players, especially his young players. So you can see why there was little communication between us. The thing was, playing for Earl was something I had always wanted to do. When you are in the Orioles' farm system you dream of playing for Earl Weaver. Yet it didn't work out. I think I was forced on him by the front office."

When Al Bumbry broke his ankle in 1978, Weaver made Harlow his full-time centerfielder. It seemed like an intelligent decision. Harlow had a great arm. He began his minor league career as a pitcher and later was converted into an outfielder. He was swift in the field and was the 1977 International League MVP, batting .335. He was billed as another jewel in the Oriole farm system. This time there was no diamond in the rough, just a plain old stone. Harlow batted .243 for the Orioles. Weaver often spoke of the five weeks in which he drove in one run. Harlow also had lapses in the field, for which Weaver chastised him. He soon developed a phobia about ground balls, approaching each one as though it were a hand grenade or a greased pig. Sometimes he wanted no part of them. Other times they slipped in and out of his grasp. The more Earl screamed, the worse it became. Perhaps Harlow needed the spunk of Rick Dempsey, who would fling equipment around the dugout when Earl said something that hurt him. Maybe he needed Palmer's wit and self-confidence to challenge the manager to a verbal war. He had neither.

Quiet and reserve are understatements of Larry Harlow's personality. He is withdrawn and introverted. On the Orioles' spring bus trips he would sit alone and stare out the window for hours while chain-smoking cigarettes. He often wore all black and his face took on the look of a haunted man when times were difficult. He never seemed happy. On his wedding day he was married in the morning and rode to the ball park with Rich Dauer and Gary Roenicke that afternoon. Harlow never said a word about the event. The Orioles learned of it from Harlow's bride during the game and threw a champagne party for him afterward. If Harlow would not announce his own wedding, it is understandable why he could not tell Weaver to back off when Earl treaded on sensitive ground.

In 1979, Bumbry was back in centerfield and Harlow was serving as a defensive replacement for Ken Singleton. When DeCinces suffered a back injury he went on the disabled list and the Orioles recalled Benny Ayala from Rochester. Three weeks later, DeCinces was healthy. General Manager Peters wanted to send Ayala back to Rochester. Weaver liked Ayala as a right-handed pinch hitter. He urged Peters to deal Harlow instead. Weaver felt that Ayala could supply a hit that might win a game. Harlow was not producing in his limited plate appearances and was nothing special defensively. Eventually, Peters agreed and swapped Harlow to the Angels.

Ironically, when Angels and Baltimore met in the American League playoffs, Harlow delivered the hit that gave California its only win of the series. Even on that night, which should have carried such significance for Harlow, he could barely smile. With the Angels, Harlow's defense improved and his batting average has been in the .280s as a part-time player. He is better than in Baltimore, but hardly the star many claimed he would be. All of this demonstrates that leaving Weaver is not always the answer to a player's problems. Two other players in this category are Jim Hardin and Wayne Garland.

Hardin was an 18-game winner in 1968. The following season Weaver told him he had lost his job in the starting rotation. The Birds were loaded with stellar hurlers Mike Cuellar, Jim Palmer,

Dave McNally, and Tom Phoebus. During spring training, Weaver used Hardin out of the bullpen.

"He started me at the end of the spring against the Yankees," Hardin told the *New York Post's* Maury Allen. "Before that game he told me I would be in the bullpen no matter what. He said this in front of everyone on the bench. He seemed to be trying to show me up. From that point, he second-guessed me on every bad pitch. I think I was treated unfairly and I can't have respect for a man who doesn't respect me . . . If there is one thing Weaver doesn't know about, it is pitching. He could never hit it, could he?"

Hardin made these remarks in 1972 when he was traded to the Yankees. After his impressive 1968 season, Hardin went 12–14 over the next three years and developed arm trouble. Weaver's contention was that Hardin's talent simply did not match that of his starters. He was a good pitcher, but not a great one. Despite the blast, Weaver refused to knock Hardin, calling him a nice guy. Earl even rented a home to Hardin. It also was because of Earl's recommendation that the Orioles selected Hardin from the Mets in the Minor League draft.

Hardin's complaints are common among those of Baltimore pitchers. If you vary from the Oriole game plan and pitch a batter your way, you had better get him out. If not, Weaver feels you must answer to him. His questions are never very comfortable. Also, Weaver will not compliment a pitcher who retired a batter his own way. That may not seem fair, but it is life under Earl.

In 1976, Wayne Garland became a 20-game winner for the first and last time of his career. He did not completely enter the starting rotation until June 15, and then he finished the season with a 15–3 rush, making his record 20–7. Garland was a free agent at the end of the season and his criticism of Weaver was widely quoted.

"Money is the main factor in what team I sign with," said Garland. "But if there was a change of managers, it could make it a lot easier for me. I am not going to make a decision based on the fact Joe Altobelli might be here. If he were, it would make me want to stay with the Orioles more than with Weaver."

Altobelli managed the Orioles' Class AAA Rochester club and was rumored to be under consideration as a replacement for

Weaver. Garland spent 2½ years under Earl. He did not appreciate Weaver's personality and felt the manager waited too long before freeing him from the bullpen. As in the Hardin situation, Weaver did not publicly criticize Garland. Considering the 10-year, $2.2 million contract he received by shifting to Cleveland, Garland would not have resigned with the Orioles if John the Baptist had been the manager. Understandably, many of the Orioles were angered by Garland's remarks.

"Earl handled Garland right," said former Oriole Coach Jim Frey. "He broke him into the starting rotation gradually, like he does all young pitchers. Down the stretch Wayne had a helluva time winning his 20th game. It took him three tries, but Earl kept sending him out there, knowing full well Wayne would not play for the Orioles the next year. I think he did Wayne a favor."

When he joined the Indians, Garland injured the rotator cuff in his right shoulder. A serious operation followed. Then there was the long and often agonizing comeback road which never led in the direction that Garland had hoped.

One player who did annoy Weaver with his public statements was Bob Reynolds. Never a particularly mature person, the man they called "Bullet Bob" had a fearsome temper that prohibited him from being a respectable pitcher.

"Players have lost all respect for Weaver," said Reynolds. "They can't stand his constant screaming."

"You can never answer a guy like Reynolds," said Weaver. "After giving up a homer, he goes up to an umpire and yells, 'I'm gonna kill you.' There are a lot of people afraid of Reynolds, and I am at times."

What little success Reynolds had on the mound came under Weaver. He ended up drifting through several organizations, mostly in the minors. He also toiled in the defunct Inter-American League.

Aside from the tone of his voice, the most controversial aspect of Weaver is how he deals with young players.

"He is a lot better at that now than he used to be," said Brooks Robinson. "He is more patient and more understanding. He talks to them more."

But Earl always expects a player to prove himself. He does not like rookies who are loud, impatient or questioning of the manager. In the past he preferred first-year players to be quieter than Harpo Marx.

In 1970, the Orioles recalled Bobby Grich from Rochester. Grich was batting .383 at the time. When he joined the team, he decided to stop in at Weaver's office to say hello.

"What do you want?" asked Weaver in a gruff voice as Grich approached him.

"I just thought I'd let you know I was here," said Grich.

"That's it?" asked Weaver.

Grich nodded and walked away.

"Now, Earl will ask a kid to come and chat with him," said Grich. "But not back then. I had always been very close to my managers in the minors and Earl's conduct confused me."

During a game in 1970 Weaver decided to pinch hit for Grich with the bases loaded. The Orioles had wrapped up the pennant and Grich felt there was no reason for the move.

"How am I supposed to learn to hit up here if you keep batting for me?" Grich roared at the manager. Weaver and Grich leaped at each other and were separated by Elrod Hendricks. Grich spent six seasons with the Orioles and learned to live with Weaver. Nonetheless, he bolted for California as soon as he gained free agency.

"I never miss a thing about the Orioles," said Grich. "The only thing I liked about Maryland was the crabs. I remember my rookie season when Weaver said only five words to me all year. In 1976, I had a virus for a week and was out of action. People stopped talking to me, like I wanted to be sick. I'll never forget that. In Baltimore, they view you according to your batting average." Still, Grich was a productive athlete for the Orioles.

The only player Weaver was not able to control was catcher Earl Williams. Williams had a short and controversial career. The highlight of it was winning the Rookie of the Year award in 1971 while with Atlanta. Weaver wanted Williams. He was the home run-hitting catcher of the manager's dreams. That is why Weaver was willing to pay heavily to obtain him from the Braves. Baltimore sent Pat Dobson, Roric Harrison, Dave Johnson, and Johnny Oates to Atlanta for Williams, who had clubbed a total of 61 homers in his first two big league seasons.

With the Orioles, Williams was suspended and constantly in

trouble. He was late for games, late for batting practice, and late for buses. He once stuck his tongue out at Jim Palmer after Palmer had shaken off one of his signs. He would shout obscenities in the on-deck circle which was next to the seats of Orioles' Owner Jerry Hoffberger and his family. During his two-year stay, the Birds did win a pair of division titles. But Williams was generally a disappointment. He even announced that he did not enjoy catching and wanted to play first base. The Orioles had Boog Powell at that spot. Williams blamed Weaver for his lack of production (36 homers in two years) and often pouted. He expected superstar treatment although he was barely an average player. In 1975, the Birds shipped him back to Atlanta for a nonentity named Jimmy Freeman and $75,000. Williams never repeated those early productive seasons. By the late 1970s he was out of baseball. His mother took out an advertisement in the *New York Times* classified section in 1978 in which she stated her son was a proven major league catcher looking for work. The Montreal Expos answered the ad and contacted Williams' mother, but Earl refused to attend their tryout. He popped up in the Mexican League in 1980.

"Earl Weaver likes to say he got all those gray hairs from me," says Jim Palmer. "But don't let him kid you, they came from Earl Williams."

Still, most Oriole players were not unhappy. They did not loathe Weaver. They were like Ross Grimsley.

"I will always be grateful to Earl Weaver," said Grimsley. "I remember the 1975 season when I started the year 1–8. I went to see Earl and told him to put me in the bullpen. He refused. He said I was one of his starters. He said it wasn't time to give up on me. I went 9–5 the rest of the season. It may not seem like it to some players, but Earl knows the value of having confidence in you and giving you a pat on the back. He loves and understands pitchers. I remember a spring training game in which I gave up 12 runs in an inning and he didn't get upset. Weaver respects pitchers. I played for Sparky Anderson, and he had no use for pitchers. I was under Dick Williams and he had no use for anyone. Earl is the best manager around."

The Orioles often tell this story about Grimsley. Early in his career with Baltimore he was struggling. Pitching Coach George

Bamberger told Ross he needed something extra. Soon Bamberger and Ross were refining a spitter and a greaseball. Bamberger called it a sinker. Grimsley was reluctant to use his new weapons in a game. One day, the bases were loaded and Bamberger came to the mound.

"What do you want?" asked Grimsley.

"I think now is the time," said Bamberger.

"For what?" asked Grimsley.

"Now is the time to use anything else you have," said Bamberger, who then walked back to the dugout.

By the end of the 1974 season, Grimsley had won 18 games and earned the reputation as a pitcher who was willing to push the rules to the limit.

"A funny thing happened in 1974," recalled Grimsley. "We had been losing a lot of games because Earl kept waiting for the big inning. You know how he loves the home run. Well, we didn't have a power team that year. Still, he wouldn't steal bases or bunt. It got to where we were about ten games out in August and we called a meeting. We talked about Earl not bunting and stuff and we decided we would bunt and move runners along on our own. We did and we won the division. To his credit, Earl saw it was working and he didn't try to change us. Also, he knew when to make the pitching changes late in the game."

Grimsley has endless praise for Weaver's knowledge of pitching.

"He hates walks more than any manager I have seen," said Grimsley. "They make him crazy. The same is true if you throw a hitter your second best pitch in a tight spot. That drives him up a wall. He won't tolerate walks and mental mistakes and that is why the Orioles don't fall into those traps. The big thing is, Earl will stick with his pitchers. It is no accident he has had all those 20-game winners. He fights for his players and fights with you. We had a screaming match that went from the mound to the dugout and finally to the clubhouse. There, we locked the doors and didn't come out until we both had had our say. But he will listen to you and he is completely honest. The man also has patience. For example, he stuck with Mike Cuellar as long as he could, longer than most managers would have."

In 1976, Cuellar had been relegated to a spot starter. His

record was 4–13 and he barely resembled the 20-game winner of three years before.

He was 39 and obviously near the end. Weaver had banished him to the bullpen.

"Weaver buried me," Cuellar said. "I have him to thank for a lousy season. I don't think he wants to win. If he did, he would pitch me."

"I gave Cuellar more chances than my first wife," replied Weaver. "I just had other pitchers who were better."

Those close to the situation agreed with Grimsley. Earl did all he could. Cuellar had run out of chances.

When you manage the same team for 13 years and the same players for over a decade, not everyone loves you all the time. It is like a marriage. Most husbands can produce a list of grievances against their wives, and wives can do the same for their spouses. So it is with Weaver and the Orioles.

"I played for Gene Mauch and now I'm under Earl," said Ken Singleton. "I'll take Earl over Mauch any time. Earl has a sense of humor. If you want to talk to him, he'll listen. When you walk into the Oriole clubhouse, you sense confidence. I did the first time I came to Baltimore from Montreal. The players in Baltimore always know they will win a lot of games and be in the pennant race. No one has to say it, it is a fact. Maybe some people don't like to admit it, but that attitude comes from Earl."

Singleton joined the Orioles in 1975 and he says Weaver has not changed.

"He still leaves most guys alone, but he won't let a mistake go by unnoticed," said Singleton. "He gets more out of his talent than any other manager. He loves statistics. The players joke about it. When Lee May was with us and we were playing Boston, Lee would walk over to Luis Tiant and ask Tiant when he was pitching. Lee knew that Weaver wouldn't play him that day because he was 3-for-35 against Tiant. He would come back into the clubhouse and tell everybody he had talked to Luis and now he knew what day not to bother showing up at the park. The book [Weaver's statistics] is always there and the players know it. The only ones who don't have to worry about it are Eddie Murray and me."

Earl Williams and Bob Reynolds are not typical Orioles. If any one player represents the Orioles, it is Singleton. He has a .295 lifetime batting average and the second best on-base percentage in all of baseball. Outside of Maryland he is barely known. He is one of the main gears of the Bird machine. He is steady, functional, and productive. Like the Baltimore pitchers who shun walks and stick with their best two pitches, Singleton keeps the game basic. After five years of listening to Earl beg him to swing for power, Singleton has altered his hitting style so home runs will be more frequent. Nevertheless, he will not swing at a bad pitch and every action he takes on the field has a purpose. Like his speech and dress, Ken Singleton the ballplayer is neat, precise, and fluid.

Singleton revels in the Oriole atmosphere. He makes quite a bit of noise in the dugout, especially when Al Bumbry is at bat. Then he yells, "Come on Little Boomer!" Usually, half of the Orioles form a chorus behind him, especially when Bumbry leads off the game.

Like Singleton, Murray, Belanger, Mike Flanagan, Scott McGregor, Rich Dauer, and others (yes, even Palmer), Bumbry is the kind of player who makes the Orioles click. To listen to the tale of Al Bumbry is to know the soul of the Orioles. Unlike Bumbry, not all the Baltimore Orioles have fought in Vietnam, but most have Bumbry's spirit. For this reason, it is necessary to hear the saga of Al Bumbry.

"I can't be like a lot of guys in the majors," said Bumbry. "I'm not a big power hitter. I'm not a great defensive outfielder. I don't have a great arm. I don't have tons of natural talent. I'm just a good player who strives to be the best I can."

Driving himself to the limit, aiming for the impossible, has been a part of Alonza Benjamin Bumbry, beginning with his Fredricksburg, Virginia youth.

"My passion was always basketball. I played baseball, too, but basketball was special. I played it all the time even if I didn't have a ball. I used to make my own basketballs out of socks when we couldn't afford one."

Bumbry is the third oldest of nine children (six boys and three girls). His father was in construction work and his mother was a domestic worker. The family was not well off. "I remember my father talking a lot about where the money to pay the bills would come from. Growing up was not easy. I had a speech impediment [stuttering] and you know how kids are. They can be cruel if you're small or have something wrong with you. So I was shy and didn't say much. The same held true in high school. I didn't socialize much or anything. I was known because I was good at basketball."

At Fredricksburg's "colored school," Perry Bunche, Al was a 5-foot-8 guard who averaged 32 points a game in his senior year in 1964.

"My school was really small. We had only 29 kids in my graduating class and that was the largest class in the history of the school. Really, I didn't know what I was going to do after high school. I was in no financial position to go to college and so I really didn't think about it."

Virginia State College entered Bumbry's life by offering him a basketball scholarship.

"Playing college basketball sounded like fun, so I went. I did play some summer baseball during this time, but basketball was still my thing."

At Virginia State Bumbry was a standout point guard and earned All-League honors, along with Bob Dandridge, who played for Norfolk State and became a Washington Bullet star. While in college, Bumbry made a decision which would profoundly alter his life.

"In 1966, I joined the Army ROTC. I had just gone down to the draft board and was classified 1-A. It was just a matter of time before I would be called up for service. I went into the ROTC because it would enable me to finish school. The Vietnam War was going strong and I was trying to buy some time, hoping things would cool off before I got out of school. I graduated in 1969 and really didn't know what I would do. I wanted to play pro basketball, but I wasn't drafted. I didn't want to teach. I had been playing on summer teams for Dick Bowie [an Oriole scout] and he was telling me that I was good enough to play pro baseball. The Orioles drafted me in the 11th round. They offered me no bonus because of my military commitment. I signed and was sent to Stockton [California League] knowing that it was just a matter of time before I had to report to the Army."

After one month of baseball, Bumbry received the inevitable call.

"When they gave me the oath, I was shaking. I knew what all

this meant. Really, I wasn't anti-military, but I wasn't very happy about going to Vietnam. In fact, I was scared to death."

Because of his ROTC training, Bumbry was commissioned a 2nd lieutenant in the 11th Armored Cavalry Regiment stationed at Long Binh, near Saigon.

"I was put in charge of a platoon of about 40 guys," said Bumbry. "I have said before that I was shy and not a good talker as a kid. Here I was responsible for all these lives. It was scary and it made me grow up very fast."

During Al's ninth day in Vietnam he caught his first glimpse of hell.

"We were on tanks heading down this trail. Usually you would never go over the same trail twice because the Viet Cong would mine it after the first time. On this occasion, we had no choice. I was in the first tank, which is uncommon for the head of a platoon. Normally, I would be in back. Anyhow, I heard this explosion. The fourth tank in line had hit a mine. My sergeant and another fellow in my platoon were killed. I mean, they were just gone. There was a four-foot hole in the ground. This really affected me. The sergeant had been a good friend, he was showing me the ropes and he had only 19 days left before going home."

Those were the only two men Bumbry would lose from his platoon. He also earned a Bronze Star during his 11-month stay in the jungle.

"We got the medal for ambushing these Viet Cong and capturing two tons of rice. Really, the fighting and jungle weren't the worst part of being there. The days were long, hard and wet, but the worst was the mental strain. You always worried that you might walk over a mine, into an ambush or something like that. You couldn't trust anyone, because the people who seemed like peaceful farmers during the day were helping the Viet Cong at night. It was difficult to keep your sanity. Look, I'm not a rah-rah guy or a hero. I just did what I had to do."

After two years of active duty, Bumbry was discharged from the service in May 1971. He was 24 years old.

"People tell me I came through Vietnam very well. I have friends who always have nightmares and talk in their sleep. They jump when they hear a loud noise, and things like that."

Bumbry was lucky. He was haunted by relatively few ghosts from his Asian experience.

Coming home, he had one goal, "I wanted to make it as a pro ballplayer." He had a week of spring training and reported to the Birds' farm team in Aberdeen, Maryland, where he batted .336.

"I was very proud of what I did at Aberdeen. I had hit well after not playing ball for two full years. Yet, I didn't get invited to the Instructional League that winter. I was hurt by that slight since all the players the Orioles considered prospects received invitations. That bothered me. It seemed like they were writing me off. All of this made me more determined. When people say I can't do something, it makes me strive to prove them wrong. That's what motivates me the most."

In 1972, Bumbry established himself as a player to watch. He began the year with the O's class AA Asheville team and hit .345. He was promoted at midseason to Rochester, where he batted .347, and ended up with the Birds in September.

The following summer, Bumbry made the Orioles and, with Rich Coggins, was named the American League's co-Rookie of the Year. Like Bumbry, Coggins was a 5-foot-8, left-hand hitting outfielder. In that division championship year of 1973, Bumbry batted .317 and Coggins .319.

Bumbry was almost lost by the O's in 1975. Montreal was given the choice of Bumbry or Coggins in the deal that brought Ken Singleton to Baltimore. The Expos asked for Coggins, who then was also considered the better prospect by the Oriole organization.

By midseason, Coggins was in the minor leagues and Bumbry was starting for the Birds.

"You know, what happened to Coggins was strange," said Bumbry. "We came up together and were the same kind of players. Yet, he has been out of the game since 1976."

Although Bumbry is an integral part of the Orioles, he and Weaver engaged in a test of wills early in Al's career.

"When I was in the minors we all heard about Earl," said Bumbry. "He was this tough guy who didn't take anything from anyone. As a young player, I had trouble understanding him. He had this attitude of 'What I say, goes.' You did what he wanted or you got out. He is not as single-minded as he once was. He wants to win so badly, he pushes you hard. When a young player disagrees with him, he will sometimes say he has been managing longer than you've been playing."

In 1977, Weaver and Bumbry engaged in their first and only shouting match.

"Earl and [third base coach] Billy Hunter got upset when I didn't score on this play from third base," said Bumbry. "Earl used to get on me about the way I led off from bases. I didn't agree with what he was saying."

According to Bumbry, the exchange went something like this:

"Well, if you don't want to listen, don't," said Weaver. "Just do what you want."

"I will," said Bumbry.

"Do what you want," roared Weaver.

"I will," repeated Bumbry.

"If you think you're right, go ahead," said Weaver.

"I think I'm right," answered Bumbry.

"After that, we learned to respect each other," said Bumbry. "He'll listen to my opinion. Earl is very spontaneous. There are times when you have to let things go in one ear and out the other. You can't let him get to you or you won't be able to play the best you can. When I was a young player Earl would scream at me. I never had anyone but my parents yell at me like that. That took some getting used to. But there are times he is going to scream. Some young players think he is the Big Bad Wolf, but he is not.

"Earl has a way of doing things and he sticks to it. He doesn't care if you go 4-for-4, you'll be on the bench the next day if your stats against that day's pitcher are bad. That bothers some players. They don't like to think they play or sit because of stats. They like to think they're playing because they're good players. But you must give Earl his due. He has a great record. He knows how to use his 25 players. He pushes the right buttons, gets the right hitters against the right pitchers. One thing I really like about Earl is that he will admit his mistakes and he will give you reasons why he does things."

Until his retirement in 1977, Brooks Robinson was the Orioles. His credentials are impeccable. He played in every All-Star game from 1960–74. From 1960–76, he appeared in 97% of the Orioles' games. Ty Cobb is the only American League player to take part in more games than Robinson. He finished with a lifetime .267 batting average and a reputation for excellence as a third baseman. Now a television announcer for the Orioles, Brooks has observed Weaver's entire career in Baltimore.

"Earl has mellowed so much over the years," says Robinson. "He used to rant and rave more. He is far more relaxed. He has changed with the times. He will tolerate those tape players some members of the team like to carry around. He never used to. In the past, those things would get him hollering. The way he deals with young players has also changed. He is not as hard on them. Early in his career Earl scared and demoralized some. It was negative.

"But the thing to remember about Earl is that most players have no trouble with him. Usually, you only hear the bad things. I loved playing under Earl. Of course, he played me every day. It was only toward the end I didn't like it, and then the part that bothered me was sitting on the bench, not Earl. He is the best manager around and has been for a long time. It is only now he is getting the credit he has long deserved. In the past, they said he won because he had Frank and Brooks Robinson, Boog Powell, Palmer, and the rest. But the face of his team has changed several times over the years and he still wins."

There was one conflict between Earl and Brooks.

"It happened in 1974," recalled Brooks. "We were losing and Earl made a comment about some guys on the team being over the hill. He didn't say who, but I got really mad when I saw it in the newspaper because he didn't have to mention names. It was the older players he meant. We argued over that for a while and then it blew over. That's the great thing about Earl. He has no doghouse. He has a fight with Palmer or Dempsey, and they keep playing. Other managers would sit a player down for a week to show him whose boss. That just starts another feud and Earl realizes it. He holds no grudges."

Weaver reveres Robinson. When the Orioles held "Thanks Brooks Day," Weaver worked on his own speech for hours. None of the words would do. But he had to go on the field and say something. Tears in his eyes, he spoke in a soft voice with long silences between sentences.

"Brooks saved my job several times," said Weaver. "He was always kind to me, nothing more than a bush league manager I was . . . I remember the first time I gave Brooks a take sign. I wondered if he would follow it, him being such a great player and all. Of course he did . . . All I can say is thank you, Brooks. Thanks a million times."

"Earl has a soft side," said Pat Kelly. "He is a caring human being. Playing for him was a pleasure. I'll tell you this about Earl, when the Orioles released me after the 1980 season he sent me a letter. It was written in his own hand and it said how much I had meant to the Orioles and how he enjoyed having me on his club. It really touched me. I still pull it out and read it sometimes."

Kelly and Weaver debated religion at length. A "reborn" Christian, Kelly was serious about trying to bring Jesus into the life of his manager. Earl never denied the existence of God, but he seemed more interested in playing philosophical mind games with Kelly than learning doctrine. In Detroit, Kelly had five members of the baseball chapel movement discuss the Ten Commandments with Weaver. Earl said he respected the Commandments, "rules are rules."

One of the funnier exchanges between Kelly and Weaver happened after the Orioles had dropped a couple of spring games.

"Hey Earl, can we skip batting practice and have chapel?" asked Kelly.

"We have to get our hitting straightened out," said Weaver.

"You have to walk with the Lord," said Kelly.

"I'd rather walk with the bases loaded," replied Weaver.

"Earl handles people much better than is believed," said Oriole Coach Elrod Hendricks. "I truly believe he would be a good psychologist. He takes time to know each player and finds out when to give them a kick in the ass or a pat on the back. I don't buy that stuff about him not working well with young players. In 1977 we had ten rookies on the team. They had heard about Earl and were worried. He adjusted to the situation, treated those guys like veterans and we made a run at the pennant."

During his career, Hendricks was a left-hand hitting catcher with home run potential. There is nothing Earl likes more than a left-handed catcher who can hit the ball over the fence.

"I used to pull a lot of balls long and foul," said Hendricks. "Earl would tell me I could hit 30 homers a year if I hit the ball fair. He'd ask me why I couldn't hit the ball fair. Didn't I want to hit 30 homers?"

Billy Martin called Weaver "Elrod's daddy." In some respects, that was correct. Weaver persuaded the Orioles to take Hendricks in the minor league draft. Twice he was traded away from

Baltimore and twice Weaver demanded the front office reacquire him.

"I would be playing in the Mexican League if it weren't for Earl," said Hendricks. "He has always gone to bat for me, and he made me a coach. He is a great man to work under."

Catcher Rick Dempsey would not exactly agree with Hendricks. But Dempsey and Weaver have reached a state of coexistence, even if it is not always peaceful.

"Earl probably fights with me more than anyone else," said Dempsey. "He has insinuated everything about me. He gets me so pissed. With Earl, you have to learn to take your knocks. People say we are a lot alike, but I don't buy that. He is the manager and I'm a player. We both want to win, but we don't always agree on how I should be treated."

Dempsey is well aware of Weaver's passion for a left-hand hitting catcher. Rick swings from the right side and is lucky to total five homers a season. He has a great arm, but Weaver hints Rick doesn't remember the signs and can't call an astute game. Then Weaver will muse about how the Orioles could have obtained Darrell Porter. The Brewers had Porter on the trading block, but he went to Kansas City. The Orioles were scared off by Porter's history of drug use. Porter joined the Royals in 1977 and had two outstanding seasons. In 1980, he entered a hospital to deal with his drinking and drug problems.

Another of Weaver's favorites is Jerry Narron. When he was a rookie with the Yankees in 1979, Weaver wanted to send star reliever Don Stanhouse to New York for Narron and outfielder Juan Beniquez. Narron is a left-hand hitting catcher. In semi-jest, Weaver has wondered aloud what type of catcher cannon-arm first baseman Eddie Murray would make. Earl also likes to talk about converting home run hitters into catchers. Dempsey hears these comments and grows upset.

"The only way to get along with Earl is to try not to," said Dempsey. "By that, I mean you have to ignore his personality and go out and do your best. Earl tells me how he wants certain batters pitched. But the pitcher may have a different idea of how to pitch the batter. If the pitcher gives up a hit, Earl jumps on me for calling the pitch. I get caught in the middle, between the pitcher and Earl. That is why you have to do things your own way.

When you try to do things so he likes you, it just makes it worse. Sometimes, there will be a situation where he wants you to hit a home run. He'll tell you so. But you know you can't hit a homer off the pitcher. If you try, you'll just look bad and get him mad. Instead, you try for a single to start a rally. Both of us are emotional people. We don't hold back our tempers. We say and do things we don't mean. But he won't hold it against me, and I don't hold it against him."

Yes, Dempsey and Earl are similar, even though neither will admit it. Dempsey is the kind of guy who has led the crowd in cheers from the Oriole bullpen. After a crucial triumph in 1979, he dumped a bowl of potato salad over his head and rubbed it on his chest yelling, "Big league ball, I love it." It is not hard to imagine a 30-year-old Earl Weaver pulling the same stunts.

"Earl's style is different," says Orioles General Manager Hank Peters. "He won't coddle any player, but he holds no grudges. He'll fight with a player, but he won't do anything to hurt the team."

"I can understand a player's feelings, but I have to step on toes all the time," says Weaver. "I try to do it as softly as I can. But if a guy messes up, am I supposed to pat him on the back and say 'Way to blow it!?' That is why I know I can't be friends with players. How can I when I may have to bench them or send them to the minors? I don't think any manager can be friends with the players. He just needs their respect."

10

Earl and Authority

The Winter meetings are baseball's version of a national Moose club convention. Everyone who is anyone is present. In the lobby of the headquarters hotel you will find George Steinbrenner and the president of the Class A Durham Bulls. Also in the smorgasbord are managers, agents, and job seekers who spent their savings on air fare to attend the meetings in hopes of getting a start in baseball. When you throw all of these baseball people together, the rumors fly and the booze flows. One executive has called it "seven days of drunken bullshit."

No matter, because it is as much a part of baseball as the seventh inning stretch. Besides, the biggest trades of the year are often made at this time. It was at the 1977 Winter Meetings that Earl Weaver quit the Orioles for a day and was on the verge of working for the Milwaukee Brewers.

The Orioles were trying to trade for a relief pitcher. One proposed deal was for Seattle's Enrique Romo. Another was for Philadelphia's Gene Garber, and a third was for Montreal's Don Stanhouse and Joe Kerrigan. The Birds were offering 18-game winner Rudy May. Each year the Topps bubblegum and baseball card company holds a party for managers. At 3 P.M. on December 7, 1977, Weaver indicated that he would attend. An hour later, Weaver called Birds' Scout Jim Russo from the party. He asked Russo how the trades were progressing.

"Nothing's happening," said Russo. "You can come up if you want."

Weaver returned to the party. An hour later, he left and was spotted by a writer.

"What do you think of the trades?" asked the writer.

"What trades?" asked Weaver.

"Rudy May to Montreal for Don Stanhouse, Joe Kerrigan, and Gary Roenicke and Mike Parrott to Seattle for Carlos Lopez," said the writer.

"I don't know nothing about it," said Weaver and stormed into the press room looking for General Manager Hank Peters.

There Earl told the writers that Peters had made the swaps without his advice or consent. He ripped Russo, implying Russo has misled him on the phone when he said no transactions were near consummation. Finally, he was taken out of the room by Peters. Those present say they had never seen Weaver in such a rage.

"We couldn't find Earl at the time," said Peters. "We tried to call him. We sent some people looking for him but we couldn't get to him in time. Meanwhile, Montreal wanted to do the trade right away or they were going to talk to another team. I had to act fast and I did what I thought was best for the Orioles."

After his explosion, Weaver told several people he planned to resign. He had verbally agreed to a three-year contract with the Birds, but no document had been signed. The Brewers were looking for a manager. Earl's old friend Harry Dalton was the Milwaukee General Manager. Everone knows Weaver and Dalton represent a mutual admiration society of the highest order. Therefore, it was not hard to guess where Earl would land if he flew from the Orioles. Weaver even told former Seattle Manager Darrell Johnson he was going to walk right up to Peters' room and tell him to take his job and shove it. Johnson advised patience, that Earl might feel otherwise in the morning. Weaver would not be swayed. He found Peters and said he was through.

"I refused to accept his resignation," said Peters. "I knew that Earl was acting out of emotion. He did not want to resign. He was upset and hurt that we didn't ask him about the trade before it was finalized, but I explained to him we couldn't find him even though we had made some calls and sent out runners looking for him. He was also worried that Rudy May would find out about the deal from the media, but I told him I had called Rudy first to let him know he was going to the Expos."

Peters and Weaver set up a meeting the next day for 10 A.M. Interestingly, that was the same time of the rumored press conference announcing Weaver's appointment as the Milwaukee manager. But after two hours with Hank Peters, Earl announced that he was still in charge of the Orioles.

"I have been with the Orioles organization for 22 years," said Weaver. "Legally, I could have signed with anyone, but I had given them my word. When you work for someone that long, you have to trust them."

Peters had reminded Earl that he had been in Baltimore for a decade. That he had a house there and had just purchased a home near the Orioles' Miami spring training complex. Also, that he was about to sign the first multi-year contract of his career.

"You've got the world by the rear, why give it up?" asked Peters.

"You're right," said Weaver.

But Weaver's ego was still suffering. There were rumors that Seattle had sent Darrell Johnson to placate and detain Weaver because they feared he would oppose the Lopez deal. The Mariners supposedly wanted to keep Weaver and his dissenting voice away from the Orioles' brass. Another theory was that the Birds were going ahead with both deals, and they knew Earl was not thrilled by either trade. Peters was set on making the trades regardless of Weaver's

opinion. Some say Earl was irked because he felt Jim
Russo's word carried greater influence than his own. Publicly, Earl did not give credence to these suppositions.

"I couldn't criticize the trades," said Weaver. "I didn't
know the guys we got from Montreal. What bothered me
was not being there when the trade happened. I had been at
all the preliminary meetings. I felt I should have been there
at the end."

"We sent [Oriole Scout] Bill Werle looking for Earl," recalled Peters. "There wasn't much time because Montreal
wanted to announce it immediately. We couldn't get to Earl
in time."

As in his relationship with Jim Palmer, Earl has spent
years arguing with Jim Russo. The deal with Montreal was
Russo's idea. "Earl doesn't know the National League and
I'm sick of him saying I never got any good National League
players," Russo said at the time. "I helped us get Frank
Robinson, Mike Cuellar, Ken Singleton, Ross Grimsley and
Mike Torrez. I wish Earl would trust my judgment more."

"It was all a misunderstanding," said Weaver. "I said
some things I didn't mean and I realize what Hank Peters'
position was. We worked things out."

It would be very difficult for Weaver to leave the Orioles. He is
as secure as any skipper in baseball, where the average managerial tenure is not quite two years. To illustrate this point, Weaver
was the only American League manager to be with the same team
from June 1, 1979 through the end of 1981. In that span, three
skippers resigned and 16 were axed. Of those sacked, half had
records of .500 or better. The Yankees have gone through five
managers in the last three years.

"I could never work in New York," said Weaver. "You make
one wrong move with a pitcher and you get a three-month paid
vacation. Then, you're looking for work."

Weaver also has shaped the Orioles' front office, writers, and
other media to his own image. They also have learned to treasure
statistics, disdain the bunt and hit-and-run plays, and accept
"pitching and three-run homers" as the magic formula for winning. They are patient. There is no panic when Weaver and one of

his players engage in a shouting match. They know Weaver's teams start slowly and finish with a rush. They say wait until September, when Earl's teams traditionally win 66% of their games. They believe in using every player on the bench and count the days until September 1st when the roster expands to 40. That puts more players at Earl's disposal, and he runs them in and out of the game like a football coach. The consensus is that Weaver employs his bench better than anyone else and his September record is good because his bench expands. The more people he has, the more he wins.

"Earl's view of baseball is not conventional," says Hank Peters. "He won't bunt. He waits for the home run. If a player is on his team, he will use him. A general manager has to keep that in mind when putting together a team for Earl. You can't give him 13 good players and 12 dogs, because Earl will play the dogs. You have to know he likes guys on the bench who can hit. We sacrifice some speed and defense to keep players like Terry Crowley and Jose Morales. The funny thing about Earl is that he will never second-guess himself if he has a player swing away in a bunt situation and the guy hits into a double play. If you ask him, he'll always say that it is easier to score a runner from first base with no outs than from second with one out."

Don't misunderstand, Peters admires Weaver.

"He has his obsessions," said Peters. "He just loves the home run. He talks about it all the time. He loves left-handed catchers. For awhile, he wanted us to get Jerry Narron from the Yankees. We showed him the reports on Narron, and they weren't that good. Earl still liked the guy. But he is the best manager around. He knows talent. He has great instincts. He is immune to pressure.

"Earl is not a pouter. He won't hold a grudge. No player hated Earl more than Wayne Garland. In 1976, when Garland was playing out his option with us to become a free agent, he told me there was no way he could play for Weaver. Here Earl had brought him along and helped him win 20 games. I told Garland that Earl may not like him, but he would pitch him. Earl never lets personalities get in the way of his judgment. He doesn't care if his players like him, he just wants them to play for him. No manager prepares more for a game than Earl. No manager thinks more about what he does. He is not afraid to second-guess himself and he will change if he needs to. There is a good reason for everything he does."

That does not mean Peters takes Weaver's advice.

"Like most managers, Earl wants to be in on all personnel decisions," said Peters. "He'll lobby and he'll pressure for what he wants. Usually, we agree on matters. But sometimes we don't. Those times, the general manager's word carries the most weight. That is why a team has a general manager."

In May of 1981, Weaver and Peters fought over Cal Ripken, Jr. Orioles' utility infielder Lenn Sakata was injured and went on the disabled list. The Birds needed a backup shortstop for Mark Belanger. Weaver held a meeting with his coaching staff and they voted unanimously to recall Ripken from the Orioles' Class AAA Rochester club. Peters preferred Rochester infielder Bob Bonner, and Bonner joined the Orioles.

"I'm an organization man and it would be terrible to say I wasn't happy with the decision," said Weaver. "But I guess the meeting me and the coaches had didn't mean nothing. I like Ripken. He would give us some offense. He can hit some home runs and that's our need right now. Bonner is a fine player, but our main need is offense, not defense."

Earl did not hide his opinion on the matter, and most of the players agreed with his choice of Ripken over Bonner. Even Jim Palmer said Earl had the right idea.

"Ripken was playing third base at Rochester," said Peters. "He needs more experience to play short. I checked with our Minor League people and they recommended Bonner and that is the way it was going to be."

While Weaver has occasionally disagreed with Peters for five years, he has been debating with Jim Russo for what seems like time out of mind. Russo serves as Peters' assistant and he scouts the teams the Orioles are to face next, along with National League clubs for future trades.

"Jim is an important part of the Orioles," said Weaver. "His reports have helped us win a lot of games. But that doesn't mean I won't question him if I have a different opinion on something."

"No one fights more than Earl and me," said Russo. "We will stay up until 3 A.M. talking about how to pitch some player or how some other guy should be used. There are about six guys we don't see eye-to-eye on how they should be pitched. Most of the time, he comes around to my way of thinking. I feel I have a better vantage point than Earl because I am sitting right behind the plate. But you have to sell yourself to Earl. I remember [former Orioles General Manager] Frank Cashen telling me the way to get Earl to change his mind is to keep turning things around until he thinks your idea is his idea. If you make something sound like he thought of it first, Earl will usually buy it."

This is something Peters did not know when he took over for Cashen as the Orioles general manager in 1976.

The team finished in second place in 1975 and barely drew a million fans. Free agency was about to start and the Oriole budget was not prepared for the explosion of salaries. Worse, the Orioles were to lose Wayne Garland, Bobby Grich, Royale Stillman and the newly acquired Reggie Jackson. Baseball was changing, and it seemed Baltimore would be left behind; an organization which relied on cunning when an open checkbook was said to be the way to success.

"The Orioles were always based on baseball judgment and a strong farm system," said Peters. "I don't think anyone in 1976 knew what free agency would bring. All we knew was we would lose some of our better players because we could not afford to sign them."

Before the 1976 season, the Orioles had traded Don Baylor (another player headed for free agency whom they thought they could not sign), Paul Mitchell, and Mike Torrez to Oakland for Jackson and Ken Holtzman.

"We needed a left-handed hitter with power," said Peters. "At the 1975 winter meetings, we had a deal worked out for Rusty Staub, but it fell through at the last moment and the Mets traded him to Detroit. During the spring we made the deal for Reggie Jackson. We were sure we could sign him at the end of 1976 and keep him for the next few seasons."

Instead, Jackson held out and did not report to the Orioles until the season was six weeks old. That created resentment among the Orioles players, who thought Peters should not have re-negotiated Jackson's 1976 contract. Some of the Orioles were angry because Peters had cut their salaries by the maximum 20%.

When Reggie did arrive in Baltimore, he was not in shape. That caused more grumbling. As usual, the Orioles played poorly in April and May. But this time, many wondered if they would snap out of it. Early in June, they went on a nine-game losing streak.

"The team looked bad," said Peters. "But I never considered replacing Earl."

Those close to the situation felt otherwise. On June 15, a story by the *Baltimore Morning Sun's* Ken Nigro said Weaver was in trouble.

"Our team is going through a very difficult period," Nigro quoted Peters. "The players and team are not playing up to their capabilities. I believe that one of the biggest jobs for a manager is to get as much as possible out of his players and keep them playing to their capabilities. I realize the manager doesn't throw the ball, hit the ball, or run the bases, or play defense, but I've been disappointed that our club does not play good, sound, fundamental baseball. This is not typical of the Orioles' or Earl's clubs in the past."

At the time, Earl was working on a one-year contract in the $85,000 range. Peters felt Weaver did not communicate with younger players. Ken Holtzman had left the team and demanded to be traded. The Orioles were in a homer drought despite the presence of Jackson, Grich, and Lee May. Last, they had just concluded a disastrous series with Kansas City.

A quiet man with his temper always under control, one who customarily speaks in understatements, Peters was the opposite of Weaver. The two men were unsure of each other. Both wondered if their relationship had a future.

"When I heard about Nigro's story, I went to see Hank," said Weaver. "I said if he was going to fire me, do it now. I didn't want it done through the newspapers."

Peters informed Earl that no change was coming. He was the manager, but the team did have a giant trade in the works. That deal would change the face of the Orioles. Peters and then-Yankee General Manager Gabe Paul had a marathon negotiating session as they sought to finalize the deal before the 3 A.M. June 16th trading deadline. When the exhausting talks concluded, a 10-player transaction was announced. Baltimore sent Holtzman ("the player with the worst personality I have ever encountered, a

cancer on our club along with Doyle Alexander," said Peters),
Alexander, Grant Jackson, Elrod Hendricks, and Jimmy
Freeman to the Yankees for Rudy May, Tippy Martinez, Dave
Pagan, and Scott McGregor. After the trade and the nine-game
losing streak, Baltimore won seven straight and ended the season
in second place.

During the winter of 1976–77, there was speculation Weaver
would bolt the Orioles and join the California Angels. At that
time, Earl's old friend Harry Dalton was General Manager of the
Angels. But Dalton was willing to give Earl only a one-year
contract. He was paying fired California manager Dick Williams
for two more years while Williams sat at home. Weaver wanted
more security, so he decided to remain with the Orioles and take
Peters' one-year contract. The fact that Earl stayed with the
Orioles surprised some who thought Rochester Manager Joe
Altobelli would be hired by Peters to succeed Weaver.

The year before, Weaver had had a vacancy on his coaching
staff and Altobelli was the logical candidate for the job. Instead,
Earl chose Cal Ripken, Sr., much to Altobelli's dismay. No one
said it publicly, but Earl was well aware of what had happened to
Hank Bauer in 1968 when another hot-shot minor league manager named Earl Weaver became an Oriole coach.

When all the guessing was over, Earl signed a $100,000 con-
tract for the 1977 season. He then took a team with 10 first- and
second-year players and won 97 games and finished second. That
earned him his first Manager of the Year award.

Since then, Weaver and Peters have formed a solid team that
has revived the Orioles. Peters did it with astute trades, and
Weaver made the most of the talent given him. The two men have
learned to respect each other over the years.

"You have to get along with the front office," said Weaver.
"Just because you're the manager, it doesn't mean you have more
power than the owner or general manager. You gotta fight for
what you want, but when the decision is made you must fall into
line and support it. I have always been an organization man and I
will always be one."

That is the reason Earl has survived with one club when other
talented managers like Billy Martin and Dick Williams seem to
self-destruct after a few years with the same club. But it was not

always easy for Earl. At times he almost could feel the blade of the guillotine.

In the middle 1970s some felt Weaver might be fired. The Orioles went from a great team to a good one. Sometimes Weaver's personality rubbed the front office the wrong way, and it was said he had a drinking problem. Earl admits he has a weakness in that area, often saying "the worst thing is a day game after a day game." The meaning is clear—the nights are free to be spent in the bars. Talking for hours in hotel lounges is another baseball tradition.

Twice this has led to encounters between Weaver and the police. In 1973 Earl was arrested and charged with "driving while impaired." His license was suspended for 15 days for failure to take a breathalyzer test, and for another 15 days as a result of the conviction.

One Oriole source claimed Weaver was trying to get fired in the middle 1970s so he could join Harry Dalton and the Angels. The theory is Weaver did not watch his personal conduct and occasionally went out of his way to step on the toes of some important people because he had California on hold. Dalton had left Baltimore for Southern California in 1972. Although Weaver and Dalton have remained close friends, this does not seem to be a fair assumption.

Weaver also was picked up by the police in the early morning of August 31, 1981 and charged with driving while intoxicated, failure to stop at a traffic light, failure to keep right of the center line, and failure to sign the traffic violation.

"What can I say?" asked Weaver. "It happened to me again. My wife usually drives, but she was too smart to get behind the wheel because she had a few drinks, too. I went out to dinner and had some drinks with my wife. If you're a teetotaler, you might think it's terrible. But in this line of work, a lot of people don't think so. It's just my lifestyle and it'll probably never change. I just shouldn't get behind the wheel."

Unlike the 1973 incident, Weaver was not criticized for his alleged actions in 1981. (Charges were still pending at press time of this book.) Earlier in the day on August 30, the Orioles were drilled 7–1, by California. Jim Palmer started and was crushed for five runs in 1⅔ innings. The Baltimore pitchers committed the cardinal sin of walking eight batters. Palmer and Earl were at it again, Jim saying his shoulder hurt. He had even brought some medical journals to the park which contained articles about his latest ailment.

"Jim has not looked good," said Weaver. "He is doing all the things he tells young pitchers not to do."

Meanwhile, Palmer was saying he had problems with the supra-scapular nerve of his right shoulder. He was upset with Weaver.

"I felt like I was on trial to answer accusations," said Palmer. "I can't pitch with this kind of pain and I should not have taken the mound. I didn't let better judgment prevail. I am not what I used to be and I make no bones about it. There seem to be two standards around here. For anyone to expect me to win 25–30 games is unfair. No one else here has pitched 3,700 innings, and I think Earl could be more reasonable when dealing with a person who has pitched as long as I have. He has never gone out of his way to accommodate how I feel. It is disturbing to read I am not doing the job and I have to prove myself."

"I've got to expect Palmer to be great," said Weaver. "You must keep producing. Jim is one of the guys who has kept me here all these years. If he can't win, he can't keep me here and we'll both have to leave."

Certainly Palmer and the Orioles' troublesome start after the baseball strike was on Weaver's mind as he left the park that infamous Sunday. He had to be wondering if Palmer was suffering from a crisis of confidence. The right-hander's critics charge Jim no longer believes he can win. That is why he does not want to finish games. Furthermore, they said his pains were mostly psychosomatic, a defense mechanism to deal with his failures. Earl knew Palmer was hurting, but only Jim was aware of the extent of the injury. More than anything, Weaver longed for Palmer to return to form. Ironically, most Oriole fans blamed Palmer when they learned Weaver was picked up on a drunk driving charge. They booed the pitcher and said he drove Weaver to the bottle. This further injured Palmer's fragile ego and widened the gulf between the manager and pitcher. But Weaver would not fault Palmer for what had happened.

"I just should not have gotten behind the wheel," he repeated.

This illustrates Weaver's popularity in Baltimore. The fans usually back him on every matter, often writing letters to newspapers explaining how Earl knows the rulebook better than the umpires and is far more intelligent than his players, especially Palmer. Earl knows he has this support and he generally plays to it during contract time. He drops hints to newsmen that the Orioles are not anxious to have him back, considering what they are offering. Weaver takes advantage of every edge and it usually causes the front office to raise his salary. Prior to the 1981 season, Earl signed a two-year pact calling for a yearly salary of $150,000.

11

At Home with His Vegetables

The 1981 season was drawing to a close. Earl Weaver was holding court in the dugout. He started talking about cork-filled bats and ended up describing his retirement.

"Hey Earl, did you see where Dan Ford got suspended only three days for corking his bat?" asked a writer.

"That is unbelievable," said Weaver. "Hell, you are better off cheating. Fill the bat with cork. It changes the composition of the bat. You hit nothing but rockets. When I played at New Orleans in '55, we had them kind of bats for a month. I hit six homers with 'em. I didn't hit none before and none after. It makes a big difference. If you catch a guy like Ford pulling that stunt, you ought to ban him for a year. That'll teach him."

Satisfied with his statement, Weaver placed his hands behind his head and leaned back.

"I ever tell you guys about my first minor league game?" he asked the writers. "The first pitch I swung at. I mean the very first pitch, I hit out. I was 17 and I homered the first time I swung the bat. As I rounded the bases, I thought to myself that I only had 59 more to go to catch Babe Ruth. I hit only one more the rest of the year. That was a long time ago—1948, West Frankfort, Illinois."

Weaver let out a long sigh.

"Baseball makes you tired," he said. "My wife says I spend more time with baseball than I do with her or my daughter. And she is my second wife. But I tell her a man has to make a living. If there wasn't baseball, we got nothing. Some people don't understand that—my wife ain't one by the way. Some people say I act juvenile with umpires and players. They say I should know better after all these years. Well, I don't think there's anything juvenile about it. Sometimes, players and umpires act like kids and you gotta get down to their level. Sometimes, you gotta go below them. Acting the way I have got me all this—a good income, a nice home, a good job. But I'd love to retire. I've been thinking about retiring since I was 20."

When Earl gives a detailed account of his life away from the diamond, you know it is the result of 30 years of dreaming and scheming.

"I was gonna retire when I was 50," he said. "But the damn inflation is killing everybody. With these prices, I gotta go at least through 1982. Everything keeps going up. Did you know that cocoa was 49 cents in 1979 and $2.45 a year later? How are you supposed to retire when the price of cocoa goes up like that, and the thing is I don't even use that much cocoa. It's just an example of why I thought I'd have enough dollars to retire. Today's dollars ain't the same as yesterday's. But I got it figured out. Between my pension, deferred payments and investments, I could get about $60,000 a year. That's plenty for me. I still live like I did when I was managing in Elmira. We have this home on the seventh hole of the Miami Country Club. Every day will be the same. I'll get up early and go out and hit some practice balls. Most guys don't take the time to do that. Around 10 or so, I'll start playing and maybe stop after nine holes for a beer. Then, I'll finish up, have a drink and play some cards. I'll go home and on some nights I'll cook dinner and on others the wife will. We take turns. I'm a damn good cook. We can go to the dog or horse track. Mostly, we'll just sit around and watch some television. By 9 or 10, we're ready for bed. When the Saturday afternoon baseball games come on, I could care less because I'll be out on the golf course."

Throughout his account, Weaver's eyes sparkled. Yes, he has it all worked out, but it is hard to imagine Earl Weaver away from baseball. He sees it differently.

"I'm a simple guy," says Weaver. "I worry about inflation. My wife and me save these Raleigh coupons. When I go to New York I hate it. I won't even go out of the hotel lobby. It is just too much. I like playing golf, having a swimming pool and going to dinner at a nice place. When I took the job with the Orioles in 1968, my goal was to last five years and get a pension. That was after 20 years in the minors. Then, I figured I'd go until I was 50. I never imagined I'd last this long with one team. But sooner or later, they get you. The only way not to get fired is to quit. There have been more than 130 managers hired and fired since I came along. That's an awful lot. Sooner or later, everybody's number comes up."

During the baseball season, Earl and Marianna Weaver reside in Baltimore's Perry Hall section. They own a modest home in a blue collar neighborhood just off U.S. 1. It is a house more fitting for the manager of the Elmira Pioneers than of the Baltimore Orioles.

"But I'm the same guy now as I was back in Elmira," said Weaver. "Oh, some things have changed, but I don't think I have. The big change came for me when I was 32 and got divorced. Before that, I was just a kid. But when the divorce came, I realized it was all up to me. I had my first kid at 20, but I didn't know how to act. I was used to depending on others. Then I realized I was the guy people were depending on. I've had to do it. Everybody reaches that stage in their life. Some before me. Some after. But once you do, you take over your life."

It was in Elmira that Earl became a passionate gardener.

"[Orioles groundskeeper] Pat Santerone got me interested in it," said Weaver. "That happened when we were both working in Elmira. I'm in the garden by nine about every day and I work until noon or so. Then I take a nap before going to the park. I love to spend time with my vegetables. Takes my mind off baseball."

Weaver has a 25-by-35 foot garden where he raises tomatoes, peppers, eggplant, onions, radishes, lettuce, zucchini, beans, and other vegetables. He also has a garden in Miami.

"My grandmother used to cook a lot for us when I was a kid in St. Louis," said Weaver. "She always made lots of vegetables. I loved them. Now we eat our own."

Earl engages in a yearly tomato growing contest with Santarone at the ball park. The two men nurture their plants in an enclosed area down the left field line.

"I sneak out there whenever I can," said Weaver. "I get [Oriole Coach] Cal Ripken to bring me a couple of buckets of cow manure from his farm in Aberdeen. I mix it up with water and pour it on. Four cow flops and enough water to fill a 30-gallon trash can is the key."

As in everything else, Weaver maintains he has won more than he has lost in these competitions. Santarone has another opinion, and his is closer to reality. No matter. To Weaver, this is one of the few games where playing is more important than winning.

Marianna and Earl share the same interests. They like the garden. They like golf and they like to sun themselves by the pool. They like Miami, where they purchased a home in 1975.

"Back then, there was cows grazing around the place," said Weaver. "Now there is a neighborhood and everything coming up around us. I love heat. Can't stand snow. I don't know why anybody lives in the North unless they have to."

There are nice benefits from being the winningest manager. Weaver has his own pre-game radio show and he writes detailed scripts. Most managers would just speak off the top of their heads.

"I'm a helluva writer," said Weaver. "Besides, I ain't ever been fired from a job and I don't want to have this one be the first."

He also has made commercials for hot dogs, air conditioners, and office furnishings. He even teamed with Jim Palmer for a Jockey underwear ad.

"I didn't take off my clothes," said Weaver. "It is just like when they started letting them women writers in the locker room. That's okay with me, but I take my clothes off for no woman! Except Marianna, of course. I want to know when a woman is coming into the dressing room."

Weaver would not remove his shirt for the Jockey commercial, either. The ad was to sell colored underwear.

"I went to them kind after Palmer started wearing them," said Weaver.

There were four hours of work to produce the 30-second spot. Earl kept his shirt on. Palmer had most of the lines. Earl had one. Several times, he botched it, saying "shorts" instead of under-wear. Eventually, Weaver uttered the proper phrase and a final print was filmed. But you can't blame Earl for calling them "shorts." That is what they are to a guy who saves Raleigh coupons, puts salt in his beer, and who once sold used cars. Millionaire ballplayers like Palmer wear underwear. Earl wears shorts. "It just goes to show that I'm a regular guy away from baseball," said Weaver. "Nothing more."

Appendix

Baseball According to Weaver

- "Nobody ain't due to do nothing."
- "Our depth is deep depth."
- "There ain't no rule in the rulebook about bringing a rulebook on the field."
- "When you ain't hitting, managing don't mean shit."
- "We have a lot of guys who have a lot to get a lot out of."
- "In order to keep doing what we've done, we have to keep doing what we've done in the past."
- "I'm either an idiot or a genius, depending on what day it is."
- "The key to winning is excellents. An excellent is a guy like Gary Roenicke hitting 25 homers when you figured he was only good for 15. The more excellents you got, the more you win."

EARL'S BIRTHDAY PRESENTS

What his players and coaches would give Earl Weaver for his birthday.

Dave Skaggs: An umpire crew which is his size so he could argue with them eye-to-eye.

Kiko Garcia: One day in the big leagues so he'd find out that it's not so easy.

186

Frank Robinson: My birthday wish for Earl would be for him to finally win a protest.

Ray Miller: A dozen rulebooks so he wouldn't rip up mine.

Mark Belanger: Twenty runs a game to keep him quiet.

Al Bumbry: A win tonight. That's what he wants the most.

Ken Singleton: A new rulebook which is interpreted his way.

Scott McGregor: A voodoo doll of umpire Jim Evans, with plenty of pins.

Rich Dauer: A cap with no rim so Earl won't have to turn it around when arguing with umpires.

Pat Kelly: Prayer. He and all of us need it.

Anonymous: Twenty-five earplugs so his players wouldn't have to listen to him.

Lee May: Nothing. He didn't give me nothing on my birthday. Nobody remembered Pat Kelly's birthday or anyone else's on the team.

Jim Frey: A true golf handicap.

Ellie Hendricks: All of his old teeth back.

Jim Palmer: A fine catcher like Earl Williams who will hit 25 homers a year for Earl.

Steve Stone: Ted Simmons.

Eddie Murray: A poster of his favorite son, Ken Singleton.

John Lowenstein: A megaphone so Earl can shout at the umpires from the runway after he's been thrown out.

Gary Roenicke: Five runs in the first inning so he'll be calm.

Mike Flanagan: Nothing. He never gave me anything.

Tippy Martinez: A straitjacket to keep him still when Don Stanhouse pitches.

PLAYING CAREER RECORD

Year	Club	Pct.	G	AB	R	H	2B	3B	HR	RBI
1948	West Frankfort	.268	120	447	96	120	20	4	2	49
1949	St. Joseph	.282	138	500	80	141	22	4	2	101
1950	Winston-Salem	.276	127	439	57	121	20	0	3	60
1951	Houston	.233	13	43	9	10	4	0	0	2
	Omaha	.279	142	506	81	141	35	2	0	52
1952	Houston	.219	57	201	24	44	7	1	2	21
	Omaha	.278	97	353	63	98	15	0	0	34
1953	Omaha	.243	141	478	57	116	16	0	3	47
1954	Denver	.283	143	541	124	153	30	2	6	59
1955	New Orleans	.278	119	392	77	109	19	2	6	69
1956	Mont.–Knox.	.237	113	417	47	99	10	3	4	22
	New Orleans	.228	26	101	11	23	4	0	0	8
1957	Fitzgerald	.288	112	354	70	102	15	3	6	38
1958	Dublin	.294	37	85	27	25	6	0	4	21
1959	Aberdeen	.200	13	35	8	7	2	0	0	3
1960	Fox Cities	.233	28	30	3	7	1	0	0	4
1961	Fox Cities				(Did not play)					
1962–63										
–64	Elmira				(Did not play)					
1965	Elmira	.000	1	0	0	0	0	0	0	0
	Pro. Totals	.267	1427	4922	834	1316	226	21	38	590

MANAGERIAL RECORD

Year	Club	League	W	L	Pct.	Pos.
1956	Knoxville	South Atlantic	10	24	.294	8th
1957	Fitzgerald	Georgia–Florida	65	74	.468	4th
1958	Dublin	Georgia–Florida	72	56	.563	3rd
1959	Aberdeen	Northern	69	55	.556	2nd
1960	Fox Cities	Three-I	82	56	.594	1st
1961	Fox Cities	Three-I	67	62	.519	4th
1962	Elmira	Eastern	72	68	.514	2nd
1963	Elmira	Eastern	76	64	.543	2nd
1964	Elmira	Eastern	82	58	.586	1st
1965	Elmira	Eastern	83	55	.601	2nd
1966	Rochester	International	80	64	.565	1st
1967	Rochester	International	80	61	.567	2nd
1968	Baltimore	American	48	34	.585	2nd
1969	Baltimore	American	109	53	.673	1st
1970	Baltimore	American	108	54	.667	1st
1971	Baltimore	American	101	57	.639	1st
1972	Baltimore	American	80	74	.519	3rd
1973	Baltimore	American	97	65	.599	1st
1974	Baltimore	American	91	71	.562	1st
1975	Baltimore	American	90	69	.566	2nd
1976	Baltimore	American	88	74	.543	2nd
1977	Baltimore	American	97	64	.602	2nd–T
1978	Baltimore	American	90	71	.559	4th
1979	Baltimore	American	102	57	.642	1st
1980	Baltimore	American	100	62	.617	2nd
1981	Baltimore	American	59	46	.563	2nd
	Pro Totals		2105	1548	.575	–

20-GAME WINNERS UNDER WEAVER

Year	Pitcher	Record	Year	Pitcher	Record
1968	Dave McNally	22–10	1975	Jim Palmer	23–11
				Mike Torrez	20–9
1969	Dave McNally	20–7			
	Mike Cuellar	23–11	1976	Jim Palmer	22–13
				Wayne Garland	20–7
1970	Dave McNally	24–9			
	Mike Cuellar	24–8	1977	Jim Palmer	20–11
	Jim Palmer	20–10			
			1978	Jim Palmer	21–12
1971	Dave McNally	21–5			
	Mike Cuellar	20–9	1979	Mike Flanagan	23–9
	Jim Palmer	20–9			
	Pat Dobson	20–8	1980	Steve Stone	25–7
				Scott McGregor	20–8
1972	Jim Palmer	21–10			
1973	Jim Palmer	22–9			
1974	Mike Cuellar	22–10			

WEAVER'S REGULAR SEASON RECORD IN SEPTEMBER AND OCTOBER

Year	Orioles
1969	18–10
1970	22–7
1971	20–9
1972	13–17
1973	21–11
1974	24–6
1975	17–9
1976	20–13
1977	22–9
1978	18–11
1979	15–12
1980	24–10
1981	17–14
Totals	251–138
Percentage	.645

100 OR MORE WINS IN A SINGLE SEASON

McCarthy	(6)
Mack	(5)
Weaver	(5)
Chance	(4)
McGraw	(4)
Anderson	(3)
Southworth	(3)
Alston	(2)
Selee	(2)
Clarke	(2)
Durocher	(2)
Houk	(2)
Ozark	(2)
Higgins	(2)

MANAGERS HAVING 1100 OR MORE WINS (thru '81)

1.	Mack	(3776)
2.	McGraw	(2840)
3.	Harris	(2159)
4.	McCarthy	(2126)
5.	Alston	(2040)
6.	Durocher	(2019)
7.	Stengel	(1926)
8.	McKechnie	(1898)
9.	Clarke	(1602)
10.	Griffith	(1491)
11.	Mauch	(1468)
12.	Lopez	(1422)
13.	Huggins	(1413)
14.	Dykes	(1407)
15.	W. Robinson	(1397)
16.	Houk	(1366)
17.	Hanlon	(1315)
18.	Selee	(1299)
19.	Grimm	(1287)
20.	Weaver	(1260)
21.	Rigney	(1239)
22.	Cronin	(1236)
23.	Boudreau	(1162)
24.	Frisch	(1137)
25.	Jennings	(1131)
26.	Murtaugh	(1115)

STATEMENT BY LELAND S. MacPHAIL TO THE PRESS, SEPTEMBER 17, 1977

In the game of September 15, Baltimore at Toronto, the Baltimore club refused to take the field for the bottom of the fifth inning, and the game was forfeited, 9–0, to Toronto. The score at this point was 4–0 Toronto and the game had passed regulation distance for an official game. Manager Earl Weaver did not have his [team] take the field because in his judgment a tarpaulin over the home bullpen in left field constituted an unsafe condition.

A light rain was falling and the home bullpen had been covered as per regular procedure. (The visiting bullpen was not covered as it was in use.) Because of winds, the tarpaulin in the home bullpen had been weighted down with blocks. These were removed at Manager Weaver's request, and the tarpaulin on the warm-up mound closest to fair territory was folded back.

Bullpens in Major League parks are either beyond the outfield fences or in foul territory outside the foul lines. Seven clubs in the American League and several in the National League have warm-up mounds outside the outfield foul lines. The home warm-up mound in Toronto which is in question is 12 ft. from the foul line. This is not appreciably different from the location of the warm-up mounds in some other major league parks. It has been customary in baseball to cover these mounds when not in use while the game is in progress if rain is falling. The Toronto club wanted the mound covered on this occasion. To the best of my knowledge, no one has ever expressed the opinion before that this constituted a safety problem. No prior complaint or protest has been lodged by a manager, player or club (including the Baltimore club) nor am I aware of any injury to a player having occured as a result of this procedure.

Manager Weaver's concern over the safety of his players is not only understandable, but commendable. It is conceivable that there could possibly have been an injury if a player had tripped or slipped on the tarpaulin. It is probably also conceivable that a player could have been injured if he ran over an uncovered and muddy warm-up mound. If the practice of covering warm-up mounds creates more of a safety hazard than having them uncovered, then our procedures should be changed. Whether or not a club has a right to *insist* upon such a change in the middle of a game, and make this a condition for continuing the game, however, is highly (sic) debatable.

Taking a team off the field and refusing to play constitutes a very serious and almost unprecedented action. Mgr. Weaver states he did so because unusual and very hazardous conditions existed. The situation was not unusual and judgment as to whether or not it was very hazardous must rest with the umpires, not with the manager of one of the competing teams who has naturally biased objectives. There is a basic principle involved here, and that is that someone involved as a competitor cannot be allowed to dictate decisions that must be made by a neutral official.

In the judgment of this office the circumstances did *not* justify Mgr. Weaver's taking his team off the field and refusing to continue to play. I am most disturbed to have any game bearing on the pennant not played to the final out, but I cannot find sufficient reasons for setting aside the forfeiture of the game to Toronto as was required by the rules.

**EARL WEAVER
EJECTIONS (By Umpire —
1968 thru 1981)**

Umpire	
Anthony	1
Barnett	3
Bremigan	3
Brinkman	4
Clark	1
Deegan	1
Denkinger	2
DiMuro	2
Evans	4
Flaherty	1
Ford	2
Garcia	4
Goetz	3
Haller	4
Heitzer*	1
Kunkel	2
Luciano	7
Maloney	3
McCoy	1
Merrill	1
Morganweck	1
Napp	3
Neudecker	1
O'Connor*	1
Odom	3
O'Donnell	3
Palermo	3
Parks	1
Phillips	1
Reilly	1
Rice	1
Roe	1
Runge	1
Springstead	7
Umont	2
Valentine	1
Total	81

*Amateur umpires during umpires' strike of '79.

EARL WEAVER'S MAJOR LEAGUE CAREER EJECTIONS

1968 (2) *Umpire*
7/30 — Valentine
9/2 — Napp

1969 (4)
5/13 — Runge
6/29 — O'Donnell
8/2 — Haller
8/3 — Umont

1970 (3)
7/2 — O'Donnell
7/19 — DiMuro
9/14 — Rice

1971 (3)
6/6 — O'Donnell
7/20 — Napp
9/6 — Barnett

1972 (4)
5/6 — Springstead
5/27 — Flaherty
7/11 — DiMuro
9/30 — Odom

1973 (8) *Umpire*
4/15 — Evans
5/31 — Umont
6/29 — Maloney
7/3 — Morganweck
7/26 — Kunkel
8/12 — Springstead
9/17 — Kunkel
9/29 — Luciano

1974 (8)
4/23 — Napp
5/4 — Barnett
5/26 — Anthony
6/25 — Goetz
7/12 — Springstead
8/9 — Odom
9/2 — Odom
9/11 — Luciano

1975 (10) *Umpire*
5/1 — Springstead
6/9 — Bremigan
6/14 — Brinkman
6/28 — Luciano
7/8 — Evans
8/15* — Luciano
8/15* — Luciano
8/18 — Denkinger
9/6 — Maloney
9/12 — Brinkman

1976 (9)
4/19 — Goetz
4/27 — Brinkman
5/25 — Luciano
6/20 — Garcia
6/28 — Evans
7/9 — Haller
7/10 — Haller
7/25 — Ford
8/24 — Deegan

1977 (7) *Umpire*
5/12 — Springstead
5/25 — Brinkman
6/23 — Maloney
7/23 — Bremigan
8/16 — Clark
8/24 — Denkinger
8/25 — McCoy

1978 (7)
4/23 — Reilly
7/5* — Springstead
7/6 — Springstead
7/14 — Goetz
7/30 — Garcia
8/5 — Neudecker
8/12 — Phillips

1979 (9) *Umpire*
4/13 — Heitzer
4/21 — O'Connor
6/18 — Barnett
6/25 — Parks
7/10 — Garcia
8/8 — Evans
8/16 — Palermo
8/18 — Palermo
8/26 — Luciano

1980 (4)
7/6 — Roe
8/16 — Garcia
9/10 — Palermo
9/17 — Haller

1981 (3)
5/18 — Merrill
9/4 — Bremigan
9/19 — Ford

*First and second games of a doubleheader.

WEAVER SUSPENSIONS

Date of incident	Umpire	Site	Circumstances	Term
7/25/76	Ford	Baltimore	In defense of Lee May who had already been ejected.	3 games
8/26/79	Luciano	Chicago	Challenged Luciano's integrity publicly.	3 games
8/16/80	Garcia	Baltimore	Balls and strikes calls, immediately after Soderholm HR in 3rd game of 5-game series.	3 games
3/19/81	Mark Johnson (Voltaggio)	Ft. Myers	Spring training— Dispute re: umpires refusal to give Earl the KC lineup changes—Forfeit (not ejected).	3 games

SPRING TRAINING EJECTIONS

3/14/80 — N.L. Ump Joe West		West Palm Beach (Braves)
3/26/81 — Brinkman		Ft. Myers (Royals)

FORFEITS

9/15/77 — Springstead	Toronto	Bullpen tarp incident.
3/19/81 — Mark Johnson & Voltaggio	Ft. Myers	Umpires refusal to provide lineup changes.

AMERLEAGUE NYK
AUGUST 20, 1980

TO: EARL WEAVER
  C/O HENRY PETERS
  BALTIMORE ORIOLES

RE: EJECTION FROM GAME OF AUGUST 16,
    NEW YORK AT BALTIMORE

I HAVE CONSIDERED THE WRITTEN REPORTS OF THE FOUR UMPIRES WORKING THIS GAME. I HAVE TALKED WITH YOU AND RECEIVED YOUR VERSION OF WHAT OCCURRED. I HAVE VIEWED SEVERAL TIMES (ON STOP ACTION) THE TELEVISION TAPE OF YOUR ACTIONS.

YOU WERE EJECTED FOR THROWING EQUIPMENT ON THE FIELD IN PROTEST OF A STRIKE RULING ON A CHECKED SWING. YOU MAINTAIN THAT YOU DID NOT UNDERSTAND THAT YOU WERE EJECTED AT THAT TIME AND ONLY BECAME AWARE OF THIS AFTER THE HOME RUN BY SODERHOLM. I AM NOT SURE THAT THIS MAKES ANY MATERIAL DIFFERENCE. IT IS CLEAR THAT YOUR PROTEST TO THE UMPIRES OVER YOUR EJECTION WAS UNREASONABLY FORCEFUL AND DRAMATIC; UNFAIRLY DELAYED AND DISRUPTED THE GAME; AND WAS INTENDED TO BELITTLE THE GAME OFFICIALS. FURTHER-MORE, UNFORTUNATELY, IN THE COURSE OF THE PROTEST YOU HIT UMPIRE GARCIA IN THE EYE WITH YOUR CAP.

AS YOU KNOW, WE DRAW A FIRM LINE IN THE DISPUTE OF UMPIRES' CALLS AT PHYSICAL CONTACT. I AM AWARE OF THE FACT THAT THE CONTACT WITH THE HAT WAS PROBABLY ACCIDENTAL AND OCCURRED IN THE COURSE OF YOUR WAV-ING YOUR ARMS IN THE ACT OF PROTESTING. HOWEVER, I MUST (sic) POINT OUT, IF YOUR PROTEST HAD BEEN MADE IN A MORE RESTRAINED MANNER THIS WOULD NOT HAVE HAP-PENED.

I AM HEREBY SUSPENDING YOU FOR THREE GAMES AND FIN-ING YOU. THE SUSPENSION SHALL COMMENCE WITH THE GAME OF FRIDAY, AUGUST 22, BALTIMORE AT OAKLAND. YOU

HAVE A RIGHT TO APPEAL THIS DECISION, IN WHICH EVENT
THE SUSPENSION WILL NOT BECOME EFFECTIVE UNTIL AFTER
A HEARING ON YOUR APPEAL. IF YOU WISH TO APPEAL YOU
MUST ADVISE ME TO THAT AFFECT PRIOR TO 3:00 PM EAST-
ERN TIME ON FRIDAY. OTHERWISE YOU WILL NOT BE ELIGIBLE
TO MANAGE THAT NIGHT.

SINCERELY,

L.S. MAC PHAIL, JR.
PRESIDENT

END.

For Release: Upon Completion of Second Game,
                  Sunday, August 26, 1979

WEAVER SUSPENDED FOR THREE GAMES

American League President Lee MacPhail has suspended Orioles' Manager Earl Weaver for three games for protesting Sunday's first game with the Chicago White Sox on "umpire's integrity."

Weaver filed the protest after he was ejected by home plate umpire Ron Luciano for questioning a third strike call on Doug DeCinces in the fifth inning.

MacPhail, who was sitting in the stands at Comiskey Park and witnessed the ejection and heard the subsequent announcement over the public address system, said the suspension will be effective Monday, pending an appeal from Weaver. The Orioles are scheduled to play a twi-night doubleheader Monday in Minnesota.

"I simply cannot tolerate Earl making a public comment like that about an umpire's integrity," said MacPhail.

MacPhail left before the doubleheader ended Sunday to return to his office in New York and Weaver was notified of the suspension by John Stevens, a former umpire now working in a supervisory position for the American League.

Index

Alexander, Doyle, 177
Altobelli, Joe, 49, 154, 177
Anderson, Sparky, 3, 90, 157
Armbrister, Ed, 127
Ashby, Alan, 130
Ayala, Benny, 153

Baltimore Evening Sun, 16, 40, 45, 56, 68, 95, 130
Baltimore Morning Sun, 54, 58, 142, 149, 176
Bamberger, George, 42, 49, 49–50, 52–53, 78, 80, 96–98, 116, 145, 158
Barber, Steve, 101
Barnett, Larry, 123, 126–130, 142
Bartell, Dick, 25
Bauer, Hank, 51–56, 177
Bavasi, Peter, 85
Baylor, Don, 77, 175
Belanger, Mark, 5, 11, 69, 71, 77, 86–87, 99, 106, 113, 160, 174
Bell, Buddy, 148
Bench, Johnny, 103
Beniquez, Juan, 109, 167
Blair, Paul, 57, 60, 66, 69, 86–87, 104, 130

Blefary, Curt, 66, 69
Bonner, Bob, 174
Bowie, Dick, 161
Boyer, Ken, 49
"Boys of Summer," 120
Brecheen, Harry, 97–98
Bremigan, Nick, 142
Brett, George, 10, 101
Buford, Don, 57–58, 60, 71
Bumbry, Al, 5, 25, 27, 87–88, 152–153, 160–165
Bunker, Wally, 97
Butler, Dick, 121

Cashen, Frank, 175
Cater, Danny, 66
Cavarretta, Phil, 98
Chance, Dean, 5, 34, 51
Chicago Sun-Times, 58
Chicago Today, 58
Clendenon, Donn, 70
Cleveland Plain Dealer, 125
Coggins, Rich, 163
Coughlin, Dan, 34
Crawford, Shag, 71
Crowley, Terry, 79, 81, 87, 128, 137, 173